FACING
THE ISSUES 1

WILLIAM J. KRUTZA
AND PHILIP P. DI CICCO

Contemporary
Discussion Series

Baker Book House
Grand Rapids, Michigan 49506

First printing, August 1969
Second printing, December 1969
Third printing, September 1970
Fourth printing, October 1970
Fifth printing, May 1971
Sixth printing, November 1971
Seventh printing, November 1972

Printed in the United States of America
by Dickinson Bros. Inc.
Grand Rapids, Michigan 49504

Why This Book

IN THE WORLD-CHURCH DIALOG of today, one keeps hearing the taunt, "Speak to our times, speak about relevant issues, speak to the issues we face." In former years the church — at almost every level, from national councils to denominational conferences to local churches — usually reacted in one of two ways: the church either closed the doors of its separatistic self tighter or it clamored for the world to consider the only real issue facing mankind — its alienation from God and the remedy through Jesus Christ.

But the church has dramatically and drastically changed. Suddenly its ears have been miraculously opened to the cries of the world. At every level, the church has gotten into the listening act. It not only accepts the taunts of the world as something that will always come, but it is now listening to the desperate cries of the world for answers that can be applied to the disturbing issues of our century.

In this listening process, the church has often found itself far removed from the issues of today's world. But it is catching up fast! And in that catching up process many exciting things are happening in the church. This new opennesss to the problems round about the church not only makes this discussion guide possible, but greatly needed. In it you'll find stimulating presentations of up-to-date and even beyond-today issues. As a guide for significant and meaningful discussions among

3

Christians, it confronts the Christian with major concerns of contemporary man.

We have intentionally avoided giving answers to the perplexing issues that are presented in this guide. This has been done specifically to motivate and stimulate Christians to examine the implications of their faith in the light of contemporary questions. Nor have we listed pat proof texts. Rather, in the "What Does the Bible Say?" sections, where the Bible has some clear principles or illustrations, we have listed these. But in areas where the Bible doesn't specifically state "Thou shalt not do this or that," we have sought to list passages that will prompt further searching of the Scriptures for relevant guidelines concerning the issue being discussed.

To stimulate discussion, quotes are taken from many sources, some of which are controversial and not acceptable to church goers. As you examine what has been said and what the Bible says (if anything) about the issues presented, you'll have to do some tall and serious thinking to come up with what you feel is an adequate Christian answer in each case. In some cases you might feel a little frustrated after a lengthy discussion with others. In some areas of life where the church has had dogmatic answers, these no longer can be held. In their place you cannot come up with any absolute answer. For those whose faith is built entirely upon such absolutes, this will be most frustrating. But to those whose minds and hearts are open to finding solutions to the issues being presented in our world, they will gain new insights into the true struggles of the Christian conflict in our society.

By first discussing these issues with fellow Christians, the individual Christian will gain insights into what the church is thinking on any specific issue. Not that he will be able to go into the world and say, "The church believes this about . . . ," but he will discover some of the problems that are involved in every issue and some of the answers Christians are trying to give. Such a process is vital in any attempt to honestly communicate to our generation in areas of concern to all men. Such discussions will also help the individual Christian discover the biblical principles that are applicable to specific issues — and also what issues even seem to stump the Christian in that he cannot come up with absolute answers.

If there was ever an hour in the history of the church in which its members were challenged to give answers to the world's clamorings for church relevancy, now is that hour. And these discussions zero in on many of these issues to help you become relevant in the world in which you must give an answer for the faith that is within you. What better way can you have to face today's world and today's issues than by first searching the Scriptures and discussing these issues with fellow Christians and then taking your answers to your world. Possibly even there you'll be able to contribute significantly to the dialog of the day!

How to Use This Book

GOD FORBID THAT ANYONE simply use this book as the basis for some lectures on the issues that face the Christian and the world. It is not in any way meant to be such a guide. The primary use of this guide is to create the mind-challenging atmosphere for creative group discussions, whether these be discussion groups during a structured church-related program such as Sunday school, or in a home discussion group.

For best participation, each member of the discussion group should have a personal copy of this guide. This will allow for pre-discussion study of the materials and time to do any additional research or thinking that might be needed or desired. The more the participants think through the materials before the discussion session, the more profitable the discussion hour will become.

A special discussion leader's guide has been purposely avoided so all members of the group will be on equal standing. The discussion leader should only seek to keep the discussion going, not to dominate it with his personal contributions. It will be his task to keep the discussion in line with the theme of the day.

Each section is intended to excite you to discuss the issues. In the beginning section of each chapter the participants will discover some of the ideas that have been stated on each issue. This is followed by the section, "What Does the Bible Say?" and finally the question section, "What Do

You Say?" You may want to consider other related ideas, texts, and questions. This guide is designed to include the questions that arise on the local level. Flexibility, in fact, is the real key to lively interaction and meaningful discussion.

The continuing values of this contemporary discussion guide will be found in the solutions to the discussed issues that you establish for yourself and that you share with others. The "What Do You Say?" sections of this guide are truly the most important. Your world awaits your answers!

Contents

Do Heart Transplants Pose Theological Problems?

CARDIAC SURGEONS, cardiologists, anesthesiologists, and physiologists have coordinated their efforts to bring about a most spectacular medical feat — a heart transplant. This has caused a great amount of reaction — both pro and con.

Some have speculated that in the next 15 years body organ banks will be as available as blood banks are now. Doctors foresee the day when extra hearts, lungs, kidneys, livers, spleens, and almost every other organ of the body could be stored indefinitely and used when needed. Others have said man has no authority to tamper with the human heart, even quoting Proverbs 4:23, "Keep your heart," as proof against transplanting practices.

U. S. News and World Report described how such an "organ pool" will work: "Seven Los Angeles hospitals are setting up the world's first 'pool' of human organs to use in repair and replacement therapy. Starting with kidneys, the co-operating hospitals eventually will transplant hearts, lungs and livers. The pool will work this way:

"Names of patients needing organs and of donors who have agreed to allow use of their organs after death will be kept available. Their tissues will be matched by computer.

"When a donor dies, an organ from his body

will be speeded by ambulance or helicopter to any of the participating hospitals where a recipient is waiting.

"Doctors say the pool will make possible a wider selection of organs, thus increasing proper tissue-matching possibilities and lessening the chance of rejection by the patient getting a transplant."

The greatest problem involved in heart transplantation is not physical. Dr. Charles Hufnagel, director of the Surgical Research Laboratory at Georgetown University was asked, "Is it more difficult to transplant a human heart than an animal heart?" He answered, "A human-heart transplant is not, actually, as complex an operation as many others that we do every day. And the immune reaction (tendency to reject new tissue) is less intense in humans than in animals". . . . To the question, "Will animal hearts ever be used in human beings?" and "What animal hearts could be used?" he replied, "I think that's where hearts for transplants will come from eventually. It would be less costly, and it would solve all the problems connected with procuring a human heart. . . . A calf's heart would be suitable in size and structure. We believe we can modify the calf tissue to eliminate the rejection problem. Of the animals most closely related to man, the gorilla is the only one that has a heart large enough for the purpose. But gorillas are troublesome and expensive to raise."[1]

Helmut Thielicke, German ethicist and theologian, speaking at the Texas Medical Center in Houston, said, "The substitution of organs by machines or by organs from other persons confronts us again with the inquiry of the essence of man. Here this inquiry appears with particular implication: Is man to be understood in analogy to the machine whose parts are exchangeable? We have here to observe carefully the tenor of the question: We do not ask — as do certain engineers of the utopian biology — whether man is to be exchanged and restructured, but we rather ask, what in man can or should be exchanged?"

In an article, "The Heart Transplant: Ethical Dimensions" in *The Christian Century*, Dr. Kenneth Vaux, professor of ethics at Texas Medical Center's Institute of Religion, makes these observations contrasting Jewish-humanitarian situation ethics, and the Roman Catholic natural-law opinions:

"Rabbi Immanuel Jacobovits, chief rabbi of the British Commonwealth, has said that the most profound ethical question regarding heart transplantation is the termination of the life of the donor . . . we have no right to terminate life though only minimal hope exists or none at all. . . . The Jewish position, of course, is based on a deeply sensitive interpretation of the commandment, 'Thou shalt not kill' — an inviolable principle that protects the sanctity of human life.

". . . Opposed to the fatalism of 'When your number's up, it's up' Christianity declares that man must struggle for life incessantly.

"Situation ethics holds that each particular person, each particular instance, is unique and must be evaluated in its uniqueness.

"Joseph Fletcher says that 'speeding up a donor's death, when death is positively inevitable, may be justified if the transplant provides another human being with valuable life.' In other words, as he sees it, the basic principle of sustaining and extending life justifies radical technique. Unlike the natural law theologians, Fletcher would say that the only intrinsic principle is the love principle,

13

and that this demands different decisions in different instances. . . .

"Christians believe that this principle was personified in Jesus Christ, who said, 'Greater love hath no man than this, that a man lay down his life for his friend' (John 15:13).

". . . the Roman Catholic option . . . simply stated, is that any violation or abrogation of the natural process is wrong; for such intervention strikes at the mysterious beauty of that divinely instituted and directed process, the origin and development of life. Bringing this principle to bear on the question of heart transplants, the Vatican newspaper, *L'Osservatore Romano*, declared that the heart is a physiological organ with a purely mechanical function . . . the natural-law position would consider radical techniques justified when they enrich and extend the life of man, provided that there is no moral violation at any other point."[2]

Interestingly, Dr. William LaSor, professor of Old Testament at Fuller Theological Seminary, Pasadena, Calif., asserts: "The transplant of the heart from one human being to another in itself has no deep theological implications. It does not mean that one man's sins, evil, virtue, or emotions will be transferred to another man's body. It does not mean that the guilt of one man's heart is thereby transferred to another man's responsibility. Theologically, it is of no greater significance than the grafting of skin from one person to another or the transfusion of blood."[3]

"In my opinion," wrote Dr. Walter O. Spitzer, general director of the Christian Medical Society in a *Christianity Today* article, "homogeneous transplants in themselves are not wrong whatever the organ or tissue concerned. This holds true

14

even in cases where the donor of necessity must die so that the recipient may be treated. However, therapeutics that involves the necessity of the death of a person creates some questions that must be faced squarely by the medical profession, theological and biblical scholars, and the public: 1) Are our criteria about death and our diagnosis of death medically sound, biblically tenable, and commonly agreed upon by doctors, lawmakers, theologians, and the public? 2) Is cardiac transplantation experimental or truly therapeutic? 3) Are the recipients being helped? 4) Who decides who shall live and who shall die?[4]

WHAT DOES THE BIBLE SAY?

William LaSor presents the following interesting research: "The word 'heart' occurs more than 800 times in the English Bible, some of these being passages of rich theological meaning. In the Old Testament 'heart' is almost always the translation of either of two closely related Hebrew words: *leb* which occurs 599 times, and *lebab* which occurs 251 times. The Aramaic cognates occur about eight times.

"In addition, the word usually translated 'soul' is translated 'heart' a few times.

"In the New Testament the word almost always translated 'heart' is the Greek word *kardia* which had given us such common words as cardiac and cardiograph. . . .

"There is no mystery about the meaning of these words. The Hebrew words are common words for heart, and I am sure that newspapers in Israel that carried the accounts of heart transplants have used these words. Likewise the Greek *kardia* clearly means 'heart,' and I am sure that any medical treatise in the days of Luke that mentioned the heart would have used this precise word. We are not concerned with the basic meanings of the words. We are concerned with the figurative use of them, and how far the person who takes his Bible seriously is justified in seeking a figurative meaning rather than the physical literal meaning.

"In the Old Testament reference is made to the evil thought and the imaginations of man's heart (Gen. 6:5; 8:21), as well as the integrity of the heart (Gen. 20:5). Hatred is located in the heart (Lev. 19:17), as well as love (Deut. 6:5). Man speaks in his heart (Ps. 10:6), meditates in his heart (Ps. 19:14) and imagines mischief in his heart (Ps. 140:2). He may have a merry heart (Prov. 15:15) a sore heart (Ps. 55:4), or a proud heart (Ps. 101:4). Food and drink have their effect on the heart (Ps. 104:14-15) — we speak of 'heartburn,' don't we? Facts and truth are kept in the heart (Deut. 4:9; Ps. 119:11) — we know by heart. Even technical skill is attributed to the heart. In Exodus 28:3 we read 'All who have ability' (RSV) ar 'All that are wisehearted' (KJV).

"Turning to the New Testament we likewise find the use of the term 'heart' in connection with activities other than the physiological purpose of circulating blood. The heart is indeed 'flesh' (II Cor. 3:3); but it also is the seat of the intellect (Mark 2:6); emotion (Luke 24:32) and volition (Mark 3:5). It is 'out of the heart that evil thoughts proceed' (Matt. 15:19). The heart of man is hardened (Mark 6:52; 10:5). The heart is the storehouse of sayings (Luke 2:51) and the seat of disturbance (John 14:1, 27) as well as of gladness (Acts 2:37). Above all it is the seat of purpose (Acts 11:23; Col. 3:22) as well as of the conscience (I John 3:20, 21).

"In Scripture the term 'heart' is hardly ever used in the strict physical or physiological sense . . . We are dealing with a word that is used over 800 times in the Old Testament and at most we can find three or four references that may specifically refer to the physical organ."[5]

WHAT DO YOU SAY?

1. Try to recall some of your emotional, intellectual, and spiritual reactions to the first heart transplants. Why did you make such responses?

2. Why do you think there was so much emotional reaction to heart transplants when there has been little or no reaction to other organ transplants?

3. According to the latest medical opinion, when is a person technically dead? Does this affect your views of heart transplants? How and why?

4. What ethical problems enter into the selection of either the recipients or the donors?

5. Who should decide who should be the donor? The recipient?

6. Since heart transplantation takes exceptional skill and much delicate equipment, it is presently expensive. Does this mean that transplantation will only the benefit the rich? What can be done to make this medical advance available to the poor also?

7. If you had an incurable life-terminating heart ailment, would you submit to a heart transplanting operation? Why or why not?

8. Would you will your heart to medical science as a donor at the time of your death? Why or why

17

not? If you would, what steps have you taken to make your heart available?

Notes

1. From a copyrighted interview in *U.S. News & World Report* of January 22, 1968.

2. Copyright 1968 Christian Century Foundation. Reprinted by permission from the March 20, 1968 issue of *The Christian Century*.

3. Copyright *Eternity Magazine*, March, 1968. Used by permission.

4. Copyright © 1968 by *Christianity Today*. Reprinted by permission.

5. *Eternity Magazine*, op. cit.

Are the "Haves" Responsible for the "Have-nots"?

2

IT IS IRONIC that the most affluent nation in the world should have a poverty problem. America out-produces all nations of the world in goods and services and at times even stockpiles its food. Yet 22 million Americans subsist at a poverty level. It is reported that sections of the United States have such severe conditions of poverty that children are badly undernourished, subject to disease and near starvation. This sounds unbelievable for these United States, the land that has been called "Christian" for nearly 200 years.

Poverty in an affluent society seems as incongruous as watering a totally dead tree in the center of a productive apple orchard. Yet, as Michael Harrington points out in his book, *The Other America*, there is an invisible culture within the American culture that is woefully ignored by the affluent. This poverty-level culture is composed of millions of people who live at a bare subsistence level. They have none of the means to enjoy life as other Americans.

In establishing a family income base of $3,000 as a measure for calculating who can be classified as "living in poverty," the U.S. government statistics reveal that one-tenth of Americans live at the poverty level. The affluent of our society hardly believe the statistics, much less know any of these

19

people on a person-to-person basis. Harrington's thesis, also the thesis of many politicians, is that massive federal government action and spending will solve the poverty problem.

Harrington asks, "What shall we tell the American poor, once we have seen them? Shall we say to them that they are better off than the Indian poor, the Italian poor, the Russian poor? That is one answer, but it is heartless. I should put it another way. I want to tell every well-fed optimistic American that it is intolerable that so many millions should be maimed in body and in spirit when it is not necessary that they should be. My standard of compassion is not how much worse things used to be. It is how much better they could be if only we were stirred."[1]

Barbara Ward, a highly regarded British writer, says in her book, *The Rich Nations and the Poor Nations*, ". . . our world today is dominated by a complex and tragic division. One part of mankind has undergone the revolutions of modernization and has emerged on the other side to a pattern of great and increasing wealth. But most of the rest of mankind has yet to achieve any of the revolutions; they are caught off balance before the great movement of economic and social momentum can be launched. . . . the gap between the rich and the poor has become inevitably the most tragic and urgent problem of our day."[2]

Further in her book, she states, "We have to be ready to be as foresighted, as determined, as ready to work and to go on working, as are our busy Communist comrades. We must be prepared to match them, policy for policy, vision for vision, ideal for ideal. . . .

"I must confess that I can see no inherent reasons why such a rededication of ourselves to great tasks would be impossible. We have the resources available; we have more resources at our disposal than any group of nations in the history of man. And it is hard to believe that we have run out of the moral energy needed to make the change. Looking at our society I certainly do not feel that it already presents such an image of the good life that we can afford to say that we have contributed all that we can to the vision of a transfigured humanity. Our uncontrollably sprawling cities, our shapeless suburbia, our trival pursuits — quiz shows, TV, the golf games — hardly add up to the final end of man. We can do better than this. We also have the means to do better."[3]

"I would say that generosity is the best policy and that expansion of opportunity sought for the sake of others ends by bringing well-being and expansion to oneself. The dice are not hopelessly loaded against us. Our morals and our interests — seen in true perspective — do not pull apart. Only the narrowness of our own interests, whether personal or national, blinds us to this moral truth."[4]

"What is the free way of life to a tribal society which does not know whether it can eat next week? What is the free way of life to an ancient society where illiteracy bars most people from any of the benefits of freedom? What, above all, can freedom be said to mean when the nations who talk of this most incessantly seem to have so little awareness of its wider moral dimensions? Am I free if my brother is bound by hopeless poverty and ignorance? Am I a prophet of the free way of life if I reveal perfect indifference to the plight of the man who has fallen among the thieves, the man whom the Good Samaritan helped while the others passed him by?"[5]

Poverty isn't a newly invented problem. It's as

old as mankind. Even Jesus said, "The poor ye always have with you." But because we ignored the problem in the past doesn't mean we can ignore it now. Most puzzling is the reality that the followers of Jesus Christ seem to remain so aloof toward this problem. In fact, conservative Christians have often been the most suspicious of any government-originated programs to relieve the poor. Many Christians get hung up on the question of philanthropy (free enterprise) and the "welfare state." They oppose welfare proposals on the grounds that free enterprise will eventually cure all ills and the age-old misconception that everyone who works hard becomes affluent.

It is perhaps a too common stereotype that in America a person is poor by choice rather than by circumstances beyond his control. Many hold that the poor are poor because they are lazy and immoral. If they would just have a desire to improve themselves like everyone else they would have the same opportunity for affluence as anybody else.

We've usually argued from an affluent American position rather than from a genuine Christian stance. We've even equated Christianity to the American way of life, the American system of government, the American success syndrome.

Christians should not be influenced or controlled purely by a conservative political philosophy in their attitude toward the poor. The problem of poverty is not merely a political one, though the answer may be unsolvable apart from political measures. It is a moral and spiritual problem as much as a political one. And if the political solution will satisfy a moral demand or spiritual standard, then Christians should not reject such a solution simply because it may be a "liberal" or a "welfare" approach.

Rufus Jones put it succinctly in his evaluation of what we can do. He says, "We can refuse to repeat the false and libelous clichés propagated by extremists, such as 'It's their own fault they are poor. If they were not lazy, they would get a job and help themselves.' We have already seen that poverty breaks the spirit and destroys the initiative of its victims. We have also seen that in spite of this most of the poor are ambitious and have jobs, but their wages are not sufficient to support their families.

"We can refuse to justify our lack of concern by blaming their plight on sexual immorality. This is a major problem, but not any worse than that which exists among the affluent. The same can be said for crime, which is rising faster in the suburbs than in the cities. More money and goods are stolen by the rich than the poor.

"We can refuse to blame the unrest that exists in the urban slums on the Communists. Communism is always on the alert to exploit any situation that will advance its cause but the best way to defeat its agents is to remove the cause for the unrest they are trying to exploit.

"These are all excuses offered by the world and are not worthy of God's servants. We are to stand for moral and social righteousness and against that within the culture which is unrighteous."[6]

Does the Bible oppose or affirm free enterprise or the welfare state? Does it give the principles that really include both approaches to fighting poverty or hunger? Does it place responsibility for the "have nots" upon the "haves"?

WHAT DOES THE BIBLE SAY?

"If there be among you a poor man . . . thou shalt not harden thine heart, nor shut thine

23

hand from thy poor brother: But thou shalt
open thine hand wide unto him, and shalt
surely lend him sufficient for his need, in that
he wanteth. Beware that . . . thine eye be
evil against thy poor brother, and thou givest
him nought; and he cry unto the Lord against
thee, and it be sin unto thee. Thou shalt
surely give him, and thine heart shall not be
grieved when thou givest unto him . . . For
the poor shall never cease out of the land:
therefore I command thee, saying, Thou shalt
open thine hand wide unto thy brother, to thy
poor, and to thy needy, in the land" (Deut.
15:7-11).

"Blessed is he that considereth the poor . . ."
(Ps. 41:1).

"He that giveth unto the poor shall not lack:
but he that hideth his eyes shall have many
a curse" (Prov. 28:27).

"The righteous considereth the cause of the
poor: but the wicked regardeth not to know it"
(Prov. 29:7).

". . . One came and said unto him [Jesus],
Good Master, what good thing shall I do,
that I may have eternal life? . . . Jesus said
unto him, If thou wilt be perfect, go and sell
that thou hast, and give to the poor, and thou
shalt have treasure in heaven: and come and
follow me" (Matt. 19:16-21).
"Then shall the King say unto them on his
right hand, Come, ye blessed of My Father,
inherit the kingdom . . . For I was a hungered,
and he gave me meat: I was thirsty, and ye
gave me drink . . . Naked, and ye clothed me
. . . Inasmuch as ye have done it unto the

least of these my brethren, ye have done it unto me" (Matt. 25:34-40).

"And all that believed were together, and had all things common; and sold their possessions and goods, and parted them to all men, as every man had need" (Acts 2:44-45).

"My brethren, have not the faith of our Lord Jesus Christ, the Lord of glory, with respect of persons. For if there come unto your assembly a man with a gold ring, in goodly apparel, and there come in also a poor man in vile raiment; And ye have respect to him that weareth the gay clothing, and say unto him, Sit thou here in a good place; and say to the poor, Stand thou there, or sit here under my footstool: Are ye not then partial in yourselves, and are become judges of evil thoughts? Hearken, my beloved brethren, Hath not God chosen the poor of this world rich in faith, and heirs of the kingdom which he hath promised to them that love him? But ye have despised the poor. Do not rich men oppress you, and draw you before the judgment seats? Do not they blaspheme that worthy name by the which ye are called? If ye fulfil the royal law according to the scripture, Thou shalt love thy neighbor as thyself, ye do well" (James 2:1-8).

WHAT DO YOU SAY?

1. Since Jesus said, "The poor ye have with you always" (Mark 14:7), would we be right in ignoring their physical needs and simply stick to preaching the gospel?

2. What is the biblical attitude toward poverty? Does the Bible support the idea of social welfare?

If so, how? Was not the sharing by the early disciples a form of social welfare?

3. Why do many evangelicals oppose national welfare programs?

4. Why is the argument that the poor are to blame for their condition and should be able to help themselves illogical and less than a Christian attitude toward the problem of poverty?

5. Jesus told the rich young ruler to sell his possessions and give to the poor. How does this apply to us today? Can we follow Christ without giving to the poor?

6. Supporting worthy causes at times can be an easy way to ignore individual responsibility. How can the church help the poor close to home? How can the local churches develop programs to help the poor in a nearby community or ghetto? What keeps churches from taking initiative in this area?

7. Can one really be concerned about the souls of the poor without being concerned about their economic and social conditions? (See I John 3: 17, 18.)

8. Why do we often oppose some types of welfare programs and gladly accept the benefits from others? Is there a rightness or a wrongness about the principle of welfare?

9. When should the church be the originator of and the agency for taking care of the poor? Should welfare be a ministry of the local church, cared for out of local church funds?

10. Since the church obviously does not have the money to support massive poverty programs on its own, should the church fight for welfare programs and lobby for their adoption by the government?

Notes

1. Michael Harrington, *The Other America*, Copyright 1962 The Macmillan Company.

2. Reprinted from *The Rich Nations and the Poor Nations* by Barbara Ward. Used by permission of W. W. Norton & Company, Inc. Copyright © 1962 by Barbara Ward.

3. *Ibid.*, p. 141, 142.

4. *Ibid.*, p. 150.

5. *Ibid.*, p. 159.

6. Rufus Jones, "The Problem of Poverty," *United Evangelical Action*, November, 1967, p. 21. Used by permission of *United Evangelical Action*, official publication of the National Association of Evangelicals.

3 What If Scientists Create Life?

In 1962, a scientist writing in *Look* magazine speculated, "In the next 25 years, it is likely that man will create life in a test tube. He will transform dead chemicals into living material that can grow and reproduce itself. He will perform an act of God."

Another major magazine boldly stated that as scientists edge closer to the solution of nature's deepest mysteries, nothing seems too wild to contemplate. We might get education by injection. Science will soon be able to develop a larger, more efficient brain. A cure for old age? Parentless babies? Body size and skin color to order? Name it, and somebody is seriously proposing it.

Recently the president of the American Chemical Society, Dr. Charles C. Price of the University of Pennsylvania, urged that the United States make creation of life in the laboratory a national goal. In scientific circles, there is hardly a subject more commonly discussed than man's control of his own heredity and evolution. And the discussions seldom leave much doubt that man will acquire this control. It is a matter of when, not if.

"Man has discovered DNA, deoxyribonucleic acid. He has experimented with amino acids and simple proteins. He believes he has discovered the stuff from which life is made. Further, man has broken the code of the chromosomes, those factors which control heredity. These codes are set down in four letters, each letter being a basic chemical. These chemicals are linked in various combinations which have been compared to a computer tape. Man is reading these codes — stumbling, but reading them.

"If he can read them, can he not also write them, program them? Cannot man then control heredity, and determine one's size, shape, color and intelligence? What does it all mean? A science report concluded, 'When that time comes, man's powers will be truly godlike.' Isn't it exciting, challenging, terrifying?"[1]

John R. Holum, in his book *Of Test Tubes and Testaments* says, "We prize life so highly that most of us suffer vague, uneasy feelings when we see headlines that scientists have created or soon will create life. What do scientists think they're doing anyway? Playing God? Indeed, life seems so wonderful and so mysterious that many people feel scientists *will* almost be *gods* if they ever create life. One person spoke of the possible creation of life as a 'biological Hiroshima.' "[2]

It must be made clear that scientists are not speaking about the creation of matter. They have been able to synthesize most inorganic and also organic chemicals. The creation of life is not in the substances that might contain life, but that mysterious something that all living creatures possess.

Holum again points out that "to create physical life, then, means to cause a certain process to come into existence which did not previously exist.

"But what kind of process is life?" he asks. "What are its basic, essential features that set it apart from all other processes? How can we judge the evidence to tell if scientists have actually brought it off or not? The embarrassing truth of the matter

29

is that there is simply no neat, one-sentence definition of life that *works unfailingly in borderline cases.* The borderline between an atom and a molecule is rather sharply defined. The borderline between life and non-life is not. . . . But when scientists talk about the possible creation of the *process* of life, they are surely not talking about creating live rabbits. . . .

"What is a borderline case? A virus is one. It cannot reproduce itself outside of some other living cell. In this sense it is a parasite; it needs a host cell. Outside the cell, in a bottle, it looks for all the world like a dead chemical, and it can be stored as such indefinitely. Yet inside a living cell, and then only in the right kind of cell, a virus does reproduce itself.

"Is a virus alive or dead? Chemicals have split one virus into principally two kinds of plain ordinary chemicals — protein and nucleic acid. These two substances are then combined in a test tube and viral activity was restored. Was this the creation of life? . . .

"I'm willing to grant that this was the creation of the process of life. In any event, it was a truly remarkable accomplishment. What was its significance? What did it tend to prove? Simply this: It is extremely likely that man has the capacity to create the process of life outside the body, as well as the standard old way, inside the body. . . .

"When I hear young people talking about the creation of life, I sense sometimes that they have it mixed up with the creation of *human* life. On occasion I have even suspected that some believe scientists are on the verge of making a man, simply by fiddling with chemicals and energy in bottles and flasks! I cannot imagine a wilder thought. Let us simply look at the problem of making one kind

30

of cell (a wild enough idea in its own right)."[3]

Helmut Thielicke, German ethicist, in a lecture at the Texas Medical Center in Houston, declared, "without a doubt man has been commissioned — in the command given with creation to subdue the earth . . . not to accept her passively, but rather to use her as material in responsible creativity."

It would be good to have some theologian's thoughts on the defintion of creation. Augustus Hopkins Strong, in his *Systematic Theology*, says: "Creation is not 'production out of nothing' as if 'nothing' were a substance out of which 'something' could be formed. Creation is not a fashioning of preexisting materials, nor an emanation from the substance of Deity, but is a making of that to exist which once did not exist, either in form or substance. . . . Creation is a truth of which mere science or reason cannot fully assure us. Physical science can observe and record changes, but it knows nothing of origins."[4]

T. S. Eliot's poem, "The Rock," makes clear man's position:

> The soul of man must quicken to creation . . .
>
> Out of the meaningless practical shapes of all that is living or lifeless . . .
>
> Lord shall we not bring these gifts to your service?
>
> Shall we not bring Your service all our powers
>
> For life, for dignity, grace and order and intellectual pleasure of the senses?
>
> The LORD who created must wish us to create
>
> And employ our creation again in His service
>
> Which is already His service in creating.[5]

31

WHAT DOES THE BIBLE SAY?

Concerning life:

> ". . . for he is the former of all things . . . The Lord of hosts is his name" (Jer. 10:16).

> "For by him were all things created, that are in heaven, and that are in earth, visible and invisible, whether they be thrones, or dominions, or principalities, or powers: all things were created by him, and for him: and he is before all things, and by him all things consist" (Col. 1:16-17).

> "The Spirit of God hath made me, and the breath of the Almighty hath given me life" (Job 33:4).

Concerning man's conquest of nature:

> "And God said, let us make man in our image, after our likeness: and let them have dominion over the fish of the sea, and over the fowl of the air, and over the cattle, and over all the earth, and over every creeping thing that creepeth upon the earth" (Gen. 1:26).

> "Thou madest him to have dominion over the works of thy hands; thou hast put all things under his feet" (Psa. 8:6).

WHAT DO YOU SAY?

1. Elaborate on the essential meaning of *life*. What is life in and of itself? Develop a physical as well as a spiritual meaning of the word.

2. How do we distinguish between life and non-life? Between intelligent and non-intelligent life?

3. Man is made in the image of God. What does this include? Does it make man a "little creator"? To what extent?

4. Does God's command to "have dominion over" suggest the authority to analyze and synthesize the basic substances of life?

5. What is the significance of Genesis 2:7 in relationship to man's continuing ability to produce life substances?

6. What is the difference between man's creation of life and our concept of the life that God created, especially the life in man?

7. Would the creation of life in the laboratory be a threat to our concepts of creation? If so, in what ways?

8. What misconceptions about life hinder the Christian from accepting the data of scientifically conducted experiments in the development of life substances?

9. If Christians specialized in basic research on the make-up of basic life substances, would they have any limitations? Remember, this involves basic, not practical, research.

10. Are there any areas of scientific research and experimentation to which you believe God says, "this far and no further"? If so, do you believe that He simply builds into nature the checks that will forever keep man from gaining certain knowledge and know-how?

12. What positive presentation can we make concerning the laboratory development of life to change the world's concept that the church opposes scientific advancement and investigation?

Notes

1. Roger Knudson, *The Lutheran Standard,* December 26, 1967. Reprinted by permission of the *Lutheran Standard.* Copyright Augsburg Publishing House.

2. John R. Holum, *Of Test Tubes and Testaments,* p. 10. Copyright 1965 Augsburg Publishing House. Used by permission.

3. *Ibid.,* p. 11.

4. Augustus Strong, *Systematic Theology,* The Judson Press, pp. 372, 374. Used by permission.

5. T. S. Eliot, Choruses from "The Rock" in *Collected Poems,* 1909-1962. Copyright Harcourt, Brace & World, Inc. Used by permission.

Should We All Get Together? 4

ECUMENICAL MOVEMENT began first by cooperation of missionary societies, Bible societies, Sunday School unions, early evangelical alliances. Modern ecumenism is said to date from the International Missionary Council in 1910. Agencies came together for cooperative planning of evangelism of the world. The Federal Council of Churches in the United States was formed in 1908 — it became the National Council of Churches of Christ in America in 1950. The World Council of Churches was formed in 1948.

Today, ecumenism has become a philosophy of churchmanship, a pattern for church relations, a structure of cooperative ministries. It has even adopted a particular approach to the Bible and to theology. It considers itself the expression of relevant Christianity in the world.

G. Aiken Taylor, editor of *The Presbyterian Journal* states, "From the standpoint of evangelicals, both those within the denominations associated with the ecumenical movement and those outside — ecumenism is virtually synonymous with most of the innovations that distinguish sophisticated religion from the historic content and expression of the Biblical faith."[1]

Since most evangelicals, and especially the fundamentalist denominations and independent churches have not joined the ecumenical movement sponsored by the National Council of Churches and the World Council of Churches, they have led in the denunciation of ecumenism. Only recently have evangelicals ventured into the possibilities of cooperation in some forms of ecumenism.

Dr. George Peter, professor of world missions at Dallas Theological Seminary, says, "I am no ecumenist in the modern use of the word, but neither am I blind to the fact that God has permitted the ecumenical mood to arise. Such a mood is not man-made, but is inherent in the Gospel. It arises from the fact that believers are baptized by the Spirit into one body, the body of Christ. This spiritual fact has been converted into a mood through numerous and serious pressures upon small, more isolated Christian groups. The question is, who capitalizes on the mood and gives it content and direction? Isolation and fragmentation of evangelical movements will only weaken the cause of the Gospel. We belong together and we must build together."[2]

Bishop Gerald Kennedy, in an article, "The Church and Unity" in *The Christian Century*, makes the following observations about church unity: ". . . bringing 18 million church members into one organization will not necessarily produce either better or more effective Christians . . . the only way an ecclesiastical institution the size of the Roman Catholic Church can function effectively is to be authoritarian. Is this our goal? . . . Protestantism has been less effective in its organic unions than in its separateness . . . I am not willing to cast aside what has proved to be effective in spite of many obvious weaknesses for a theory which has proved to be short on results where it has been tested. . . . It may be that in some places the best procedure will be the creation of a united church. But to say that this condition must prevail everywhere is like saying that America should insist that every people copy its form of government, think its thoughts and accept its attitudes.

"We need to strengthen our local councils of churches and the National Council. However, I will strenuously oppose any interpretation of the National Council of Churches as *the* church . . . It is nothing of the kind and those who try to push it in that direction will destroy it. . . . But, before we talk about federations or community churches, let us face the fact that in comparison with their potential they are amazingly ineffective."[3]

Even the Roman Catholics find areas in which they have considerable agreement with Protestants — and express a sincere desire to cooperate wherever possible. This is portrayed by Father R. O'Connell, professor at St. Thomas College, St. Paul, in *The Catholic Bulletin,* "It seems to me that we Catholics share a good deal of the Protestantism represented by Dr. Billy Graham. After all, he preaches about a supernatural God, about the cross and redemption; he pleads for more faith and more prayer and for harmonious and graceful Christian living. He does not confuse Christianity and psychology, and saturated as he is in the Bible, he knows that the Christian must aid widows and orphans in their tribulation but also keep himself unspotted from the world. Surely, we have a starting point for discussion with Dr. Graham which we do not have with the God-Is-Dead crowd or the cocktail theologians."[4]

Reuel Lemmons, editor of *Firm Foundation* wrote on the subject of "Possibly We Can Get Together" in the September 1, 1967 issue of *Chris-*

tianity Today. He made these observations: "Many approaches to unity have proposed an organization that would make room for all the diversity possible. This approach is wrong, because unity is found in faith, not in machinery. If we had a common faith, we would have unity. Our great diversity results from our lack of a common faith. On the single item about which we all believe the same thing, we already have unity. We will have more only when we believe the same thing at more points. Unity does not come from merging organizations; it comes from merging faith.

"Therefore there will be no cause for excitement about attempts to get together until we show a willingness to reason together. Unity will become real when various faiths melt into one. When that happens, unity will be automatic. Biblical faith comes from only one source — the Word of God (Rom. 10:17). Christendom is divided because it has been unwilling to go to that one source of its faith. . . .

"How can we do something about unity? First we must find where biblical unity lies. Merging ecclesiastical machinery and cutting across party lines is not a step in the right direction. We do not need to cross party lines; we need to remove them. So long as a unity cry recognizes party lines and pleads that we ignore them, it circumvents the very thing that made a plea for unity necessary. . . .

"Party loyalties have kept professing followers of Jesus following something other than Jesus. It is these party loyalties that nullify our cries for unity. Retaining them will make unity impossible. Only when they are surrendered completely, and all partyism has melted into the very being and reality of Jesus Christ can the Church be one.

Crossing party lines or ignoring party differences is no substitute for the eliminating of them.

"The Lord does not require that we give up any truth we may ever have had. He does ask us to give up any error we have. Possibly we can get together. But it can happen only when each of us is willing to give up any error he may have to walk in the light of the more noble truth that his neighbor may have, or that the Bible most surely teaches."[5]

WHAT DOES THE BIBLE SAY?

"Neither pray I for these alone, but for them also which shall believe on me through their word; That they all may be one; as thou, Father, art in me, and I in thee, that they also may be one in us: that the world may believe that thou hast sent me. And the glory which thou gavest me I have given them; that they may be one, even as we are one: I in them, and thou in me, that they may be made perfect in one; and that the world may know that thou hast sent me, and hath loved them, as thou hast loved me" (John 17:20-23).

"A new commandment I give unto you, That ye love one another; as I have loved you, that ye also love one another. By this shall all men know that ye are my disciples, if ye have love one to another" (John 13:34-35).

"For as the body is one, and hath many members, and all the members of that one body, being many are one body: so also is Christ. For by one Spirit are we all baptized into one body, whether we be Jews or Gentiles, whether we be bond or free; and have been all made to drink into one Spirit. For the body is not one member, but many. If the foot shall say, Because I am not the hand, I am not of the body; is it therefore not of the body? And if the ear shall say, Because I am not the eye, I am not of the body; is it therefore not of the body? If the whole body were an eye, where were the hearing? If the whole were hearing, where were the smelling? But now hath God set the members every one of them in the body, as it hath pleased him. And if they were all one member, where were the body? But now are they many members, yet but one body" (I Cor. 12:12-20).

"Endeavoring to keep the unity of the Spirit in the bond of peace. There is one body, and one Spirit, even as ye are called in one hope of your calling; One Lord, one faith, one baptism, One God and Father of all, who is above all, and through all, and in you all" (Eph. 4:3-6).

"But speaking the truth in love, may grow up into him in all things, which is the head, even Christ; from whom the whole body fitly joined together and compacted by that which every joint supplieth, according to the effectual working in the measure of every part, maketh increase of the body unto the edifying of itself in love" (Eph. 4:15, 16).

"For as we have many members in one body, and all members have not the same office: So we, being many, are one body in Christ, and every one members one of another" (Rom. 12:4, 5).

WHAT DO YOU SAY?

1. Since the ecumenical movement was started with an evangelical emphasis, why did evangelicals so readily abandon the movement?

2. Why do many evangelicals always feel that they have to protect themselves from contacts with Christians who do not believe the same as they do?

3. Since most evangelicals have abandoned the ecumenical movement, what are the prospects of ever entering it again? Do we want to pursue these prospects? Why?

4. If it isn't desirable to join the ecumenical movement on a national scale, could a local church cooperate on a local level in a community?

5. Can a church or individual cooperate with ecumenical causes without compromising its or his faith? Give examples.

6. Should an evangelical pastor be free to attempt a ministry in the local ministerial council?

7. What can evangelicals do to reverse some of the trends within the ecumenical movements? Should they join an anti-ecumenical movement?

8. What can evangelicals do from a positive viewpoint to counteract the unacceptable tendencies of the ecumenical movement?

9. How can evangelicals get the world-at-large to realize that the National Council of Churches of Christ in America does not speak for all the Christians in the country?

10. How has the ecumenical movement been helpful to your local church? to your denomination? In what ways has it hindered these two

representations of the work of Christ? Give examples.

11. What presently divides most evangelicals so that they don't even cooperate in any significant endeavors?

12. What can we begin to do to break the barriers that exist even between evangelical groups, much less between evangelical groups and the National Council of Churches?

13. Wouldn't it be advantageous to join some of the ecumenical organizations either on a local or national basis so that we could express our concerns and change the organizations slowly from the inside?

14. Many relief agencies have a tie-in with ecumenical organizations. Should we cooperate with these agencies to help needy people if it does not involve any compromise of our theological tenets?

Notes

1. *The Presbyterian Journal*, July 17, 1968. Used by permission of the *Presbyterian Journal*, Weaverville, N.C.

2. George Peters, as quoted in *World Vision*.

3. Copyright 1961 Christian Century Foundation. Reprinted by permission from the February 8, 1961 issue of *The Christian Century*.

4. Marvin R. O'Connell, *The Catholic Bulletin*.

5. Copyright © 1967 by *Christianity Today*. Reprinted by permission.

Therapeutic Abortion: Right or Wrong? 5

ABOUT 10,000 THERAPEUTIC ABORTIONS are performed every year in the United States. It is estimated on top of that, about 200,000 to 1.2 million illegal abortions are performed. (The majority of these are performed by "underworld" hacks, medical butchers who have a meager amount of gynecological training. Some women even try to perform abortions on themselves.) Such statistics plainly show that the laws and perhaps even moral codes are out of step with actual practice. Therapeutic abortion is a complex problem that society has not solved. Within that society the church has provided little help or direction. Perhaps the church has even clouded the issues by its often rigid theological-moralistic stand, and its failure to approach the issue from a broader perspective.

The central theological question related to the problem of abortion is whether the unborn fetus is a living person with full rights of life. The problem is academic as well as theological. No one for absolute certainty can determine the precise moment when a human being comes into existence. There are at least five views: Human life begins (1) at the moment of conception (Roman Catholic view), (2) when life or "quickening" is felt by the mother, (3) when the fetus could survive outside the mother's womb — about seven months, (4) at birth, and (5) sometime after birth.

In the United States, abortion laws have come increasingly under attack. Many feel that most of today's abortion laws are outdated. They deride the fact that such laws are based on out-moded theological and sociological customs, claiming such laws ignore the complex problems of our modern world.

Nancy Hardesty, in *Eternity* magazine points up some of the critical questions at issue for Christians: "Do we as Christians have a right to impose whatever view we hold on others? If we as Christians feel that we would have the resources to cope with an unwanted or deformed child, do we have the right to require others to have such a child when they do not have our spiritual resources? Is a non-viable fetus more valuable than the other children who demand a mother's attention? Is termination of a pregnancy preferable to bringing a child into what has little chance of being a happy life? Is it even fair to compel it to stay nine months in the womb of a mother who can communicate to it even there that she wishes it were dead?

"Do we have the right to force a woman who has gone through the horrible experience of being raped to bear in her body for nine months a growing reminder of that horror?"[1]

Answers to these and other questions are not easy. Scripture is silent on the direct question of abortion. Perhaps the closest Scripture passage related to the subject is Exodus 21:22-25, in which the writer implies that the fetus is not considered human. Only a fine is recommended for a miscarriage, but "life for life" if anything should happen to the woman. No "life" is demanded for the death of the fetus.

On the other hand, Scripture seems to indicate that human life exists sometime during pregnancy.

Psalm 139:13-15 says, "For thou didst form my inward parts, thou didst cover me in my mother's womb . . . My frame was not hidden from thee, when I was made in secret and curiously wrought in the lowest parts of the earth." Professor Paul K. Jewett, in *Christianity Today*, comments that, "the psalmist is principally concerned to confess the divine omniscience. Even before he knew God, God knew him; even before his eyes opened on the light of day, while he was still being marvelously formed in the womb, God was there. But though the thrust of the passage is principally to confess a truth about God, it tacitly confesses a truth about the psalmist, namely that he regards himself as having been a self even before he was conscious of himself. I, the person, was covered by thy hand, Oh, Lord, in my mother's womb; I was made in secret and curiously wrought in the inner recesses of my mother's body. While this gives us no precise information about the relation of the soul to the fetus, it seems that the psalmist did not think of his humanity as uniquely tied to the moment of birth. The events leading up to birth are a kind of primal history of the self."[2]

The silence of Scripture on matters related to prenatal life forces us to speculate, draw opinions, and make inferences. The issues, however, are vitally real to those who are confronted with the prospect of a deformed or demented child, or a baby resulting from rape or incest. Such personal, emotional, and health problems of a mother can be overwhelming. The social consequences of these situations raise even more problems: Who will care for any unwanted children? What is the responsibility of the state for children born as the result of incest or rape? What should be the role of the church? Finding moral and practical answers to such questions is no easy task for the state, for the individual, or for the church. Yet both ethical and moral guidelines must be formulated.

John Scanzoni, writing in the *Christian Medical Society Journal* (Sept-Oct, 1968), said that Christians ought not to impose their views on society as a whole: "Regardless of his own personal beliefs and behavior, the Christian ought not to oppose the liberalizing of laws on sterilization and abortion. . . . In cases of rape, incest or disease that might lead to physical and/or mental deformity, the right to abortion cannot be denied. Likewise, the alarming increases in illegitimacy in our own society could be sharply curtailed if abortion and sterilization were readily available. It is not that the Christian condones premarital sex but unless and until the majority of people adopt a Christian sex ethic, something must be done immediately to relieve the conditions which spawn the cycle of poverty, the ghettoes, and the ensuing misery and urban violence. The same threat of overpopulation among the underprivileged affects not only the U.S., but the whole world. And infinitely more important is the right of the child himself to be a *wanted* child. It is the rejected child who in turn often rejects society and brings grief to both it and himself."[3]

What guidelines can Christians offer in the light of such an issue as this? Some consider it primarily one of personal freedom, holding that moral decisions are neither right or wrong — only free or not free. Others emphasize love as the chief factor. Concern for a person's condition may decide whether a mother or child is saved. Love for an existing person is the vital question in such a case. The absolute moralist takes Scripture simply and says "thou shalt not kill" and that's that, therefore abortion is wrong under any condition.

Robert D. Visscher, an obstetrician and gynecologist, writing in *Christianity Today*, combines these views into what he calls the Scriptural view. He says, "although love is the primary guiding principle of conduct, it must relate to the commandments and other biblical guidelines. Scripture declares that love and law are not opposites but rather are supplements of each other. Just as love motivated God to give laws for man's welfare, so the person who truly loves God tries to keep these commandments. Love subjectively experienced and humanly interpreted, though superior to cold law, is inferior to divine love objectively revealed through Christ and the Word."[4]

"The Christian physician who is asked to perform an abortion will seek to discover the will of God in this as in every other area of life. He needs divine guidance for himself in his practice and for counseling his patients. The physician, in making a decision regarding abortion, should take into account the following principles: (1) The human fetus is not merely a mass of cells or an organic growth. At the most, it is an actual human life or at the least, a potential and developing human life. For this reason the physician will exercise great caution in advising an abortion. (2) The Christian physician will advise induced abortion only to safeguard greater values sanctioned by Scripture. These values should include individual health, family welfare, and social responsibility. (3) From the moment of birth, the infant is a human being with all the rights which Scripture accords to all human beings; therefore infanticide under any circumstances must be condemned."[5]

WHAT DOES THE BIBLE SAY?

"If men strive, and hurt a woman with child, so that her fruit depart from her, and yet no mischief follow: he shall be surely punished, according as the woman's husband will lay upon him; and he shall pay as the judges determine. And if any mischief follow, then thou shalt give life for life, Eye for eye, tooth for tooth, hand for hand, foot for foot, Burning for burning, wound for wound, stripe for stripe" (Exod. 21:22-25).

"For thou hast possessed my reins: thou hast covered me in my mother's womb. I will praise thee; for I am fearfully and wonderfully made: marvelous are thy works; and that my soul knoweth right well. My substance was not hid from thee, when I was made in secret, and curiously wrought in the lowest parts of the earth" (Ps. 139:13-15).

"Hast thou faith? have it to thyself before God. Happy is he that condemneth not himself in that thing which he alloweth. And he that doubteth is damned if he eat, because he eateth not of faith: for whatsoever is not of faith is sin" (Rom. 14:22, 23).

It is interesting to note that abortion is not one of those sins mentioned in the catalog of sins (cf. Gal. 5:19-21, Eph. 5:3-5, Col. 3:5, Rom. 1:24-26) and seems to be one of those issues that fall into the realm of Christian liberty.

48

WHAT DO YOU SAY?

1. How does one's view of when life begins affect his views of the morality or immorality of abortion?

2. If abortion is considered wrong in principle on the basis of destroying potential life, would such an attitude hold true if it were known that the child to be born would be dead, deformed, or demented?

3. Does the biblical allusion to abortion in Exodus 21 concerning the accidental miscarriage actually imply that the writer didn't consider the fetus as valuable as the life of the woman?

4. In the light of seeming biblical silence on this issue, can a Christian force any negative attitude on the world concerning abortion?

5. Since the Bible doesn't treat this subject directly, would it be better for the Christian simply to take a neutral position?

6. What are some Christian guidelines that need to be followed in considering individual cases of abortion?

7. When would abortion be right in the life of the Christian woman? Is it possible that it could be right for the non-Christian in a similar circumstance?

8. How would Christian love and concern determine one's attitude toward abortion of a potentially deformed baby, a child of incest or rape?

9. What is the responsibility of the church in cases of children that would be born as the result of rape?

10. Can you absolutely condemn abortion without condemning contraception?

Notes

1. Nancy Hardesty, "Should Anyone Who Wants an Abortion Have One?" *Eternity Magazine,* June, 1967, p. 34. Used by permission of *Eternity Magazine.*

2. Copyright © by *Christianity Today,* November 8, 1968, p. 8. Reprinted by permission.

3. From the book, *Birth Control and the Christian.* Copyright 1968 by Tyndale House Publishers. Used by permission.

4. Robert D. Visscher, "Therapeutic Abortion: Blessing or Murder?" Copyright © by *Christianity Today,* September 27, 1968. Reprinted by permission.

5. *Ibid.*

Will the Medium Change the Message? 6

GOD GAVE US FIVE SENSES — sight, hearing, taste, smell, feeling. Generally, one of these senses dominates any given experience, either to make it pleasurable or unpleasant. Marshall McLuhan, noted cultural philosopher and professor of literature at the University of Toronto, says that people adapt themselves to their surroundings by seeking a balance of their five senses. Thus they can live normally and enjoyably within their environment.

We smell food being cooked in the kitchen. This excites our hunger. But in a restaurant the proprietor has carefully blended attractions that involve our other senses. Soft music appeals to our sense of hearing; comfortable seating appeals to our sense of feeling; dimmed lights appeal to our sense of sight; and small portions of especially selected foods, called appetizers, appeal to our taste buds.

A loud unexpected blast occurs down the street — we both see the flash of bright light and hear the boom. Probably our first reaction is to try to cover our eyes or ears because they are pained. But at a Fourth of July fireworks display these two aspects of appeal to our senses of sight and hearing are carefully blended, not to shock but to entertain us. We go away satisfied even though the total candlepower of the fireworks and the total decibles of sound are far greater than the down-the-street blast, the difference being in the arrangement in the appeals to our eyes and ears.

McLuhan asserts that major technological changes have been able to upset the balance among the senses. This technology has so pervaded our environment that we often aren't aware of its influences upon us. Modern man's understanding of his world is being conditioned by the new kinds of media. McLuhan underscores this to such an extent that he says that the medium of communication has usurped the importance of the message itself.

Robert Sylwester, writing in *Interaction Magazine* on the subject of "The Cool World of Marshall McLuhan," made these observations: "Our youths are of a different world. They are growing up in a culture that is rapidly returning to the kind of tribal setting of the preprinting-press days. They live in a world where 100 million people learned of President Kennedy's assassination within half an hour. They live in a world where families watch death and destruction televised on the evening news and then sit down to supper, seemingly unmoved.

"Young people use telephones differently than we do. We get our business done and then hang up. Our children visit by phone. They use the phone to eliminate space so they can — via the phone — live next door to their friends. . . Our children will probably use the phone the way we use the mail.

"McLuhan suggests, then, that we're living in a sort of global village, that electronic media draw us together in the same subjective and emotional way that village gossip did in the years before the printing press — and still does in small communities everywhere.

"All this suggests that the *content* of much of what we say is less important than the *act of communication* itself — much as when friends visit. We tend to watch TV, not a specific program. We listen to the radio, not the special song. We read newspapers, not a particular news item. Communication media have become such a part of our environment that we are hardly aware of them. They are a part of the whole picture — whether they communicate anything important or not. And so media have gone beyond their former role as carrier of messages to become the messages themselves. The medium *is* the message."[1]

Since modern man's understanding is being conditioned by a new kind of communication, printed words with their traditional logical force no longer form the basic means by which man formulates his intellectual and moral values. The electronic age has focused man's attention from written word to an interaction of visual and auditory perception. Radio and TV for instance have made the spoken word more forceful than ever. TV by its visual presentation has eclipsed the impact of the spoken word.

The new media, in contrast to printed media, involve man more totally in his environment. In the older media there were always words in between the understanding of the individual and the event itself. Printed words were the vehicle to understanding a concept or event. Because of man's experience with the new media the printed word in effect has become a barrier to understanding.

McLuhan distinguishes between "hot" and "cold" media. Hot media are those which communicate a mass of data through our eyes and minds only. They involve only one sense at a time. Cold media involve all the senses, to the point of feeling participation. The new media involve more interaction and participation of the human senses. This, in effect, is a return to early tribal culture, where communication took place primarily by sight, sound, and touch in participation.

Therefore, concludes McLuhan and his followers, because the medium is now for all practical purposes the message, we must seek to communicate on this basis. The outcome, of course, is that printed (or "hot") media should take a secondary roll in the learning task. The authority of words by themselves thus becomes secondary.

Among the many conclusions that are drawn from McLuhan's theses is his primary thrust that educational reforms are fundamental. Man is not educated if he is only well-read. He must be literate by means of all media because truth is multisensory. The new media of television, films, and computers should be basic components of every curriculum. Christians might do well to probe the implications of these conclusions on the effectiveness of religious education, and the possible need for change in present Christian educational approaches.

Yet they must take note of the implications of McLuhan's thinking on Christian thought. Some have taken McLuhan's theses as a basis for further dilution of the Christian message. Since logical thought and the written word no longer hold an effective sway over men's minds, the Christian message needs a new presentation that diminishes content. With the demise of words goes the demise of content. Therefore the Christian message must become impressionistic. Through drama, art, music, whatever — it must produce an effect in those who participate. The effect need not be mental or climactic (as in regeneration or repentance) but rather motivational. It must move men to action (perhaps for a good cause).

For many who have long ago abandoned the historical and traditional "content" of the Christian message, McLuhan fits in well. McLuhan gives new meaning to those who stress liturgical expression for religious experience without stressing the content of the Christian evangel. This is not to say that liturgical expression is wrong or undesirable, for a good amount of liturgical expression bears a vital Christian message.

Can McLuhan's idea have a vitalizing role in transforming the various forms of religious expression into more meaningful and pertinent experience? Evangelicals, perhaps, should take McLuhan more seriously. Not that the content of the Christian message needs to be changed, but so it can be understood. McLuhan may have done the evangelical a favor by pointing out the poverty and drawbacks of the old media. While he might carry his theses further than most evangelicals would go, he makes a significant point. The message isn't all words, especially traditional words and formulas.

The evangelical message is a living one. It is not one to be locked up in cold type. The Evangel Himself was called the Word who was touched, handled, and seen (I John 1:1, 2). He Himself was the Message and the Messenger.

One evangelical, Fred Pearson, writing in *Eternity*, says, "Our doctrinal view of the Bible (from the word *biblos*, meaning book) and its inspiration has become more and more mechanical. Thus we make Bible-reading into a scheduled obligation, losing its spontaneity. To use McLuhan's term, we see it as a hot medium.

"But the Bible was meant to be a very 'cool' medium. It is full of direct, passionate utterances. It conveys lust, viciousness, exaltation, hilarity, despair, and other tangy emotions. But such pungent emotional utterances are dangerous to the social equilibrium of a mechanistic print culture. They seldom show up in our approved Bible courses and are somehow filtered out of theology's scientific formulas."[2]

The Bible has become a dead book to many Christians. It is no longer alive and vital to them. Can new translations and paraphrases help the problem? Or is some other means or "media" necessary? Is the medium really the message?

William D. Thompson, Associate Professor of Homiletics and Speech at Eastern Baptist Seminary, said, "Whether McLuhan is right or wrong is of little consequence. The point is that he has begun to provoke us to re-examine communication in terms of the Big Picture. He is also helping to rescue us from the linear, fragmentary, compartmentalized thinking which has obscured our exciting, 'now,' all-at-once Bible. Furthermore, his insight into the total involvement brought about by TV helps us to understand the generational gap which plagues the Church."[3]

Yet other evangelicals do not share such positive thoughts. Arthur F. Glasser, Director for North America Overseas Missionary Fellowship comments, "Apart from an occasional flash of insight, McLuhanism is unadulterated bunk to the evangelical. His repudiation of written symbols in communication in favor of electronic impluses is a repudiation of rational men. . . . McLuhan wants us to be emancipated, contending that our minds are not as trustworthy as our more animalistic senses. Absurd!

"When McLuhan observes that 'our cultural values are tribal values,' and points out that what men want above all else is to be 'with it,' he is saying something that is true but tragic. When people hanker for the lowest common denominator of the group, they abdicate their privilege and responsibility to function as individuals, self-confident and assured. When did God ordain the mob as the measure of all things?"[4]

WHAT DOES THE BIBLE SAY?

"The heavens declare his righteousness, and all the people see his glory" (Ps. 97:6).

"The heavens declare the glory of God; and the firmament showeth his handiwork. Day unto day uttereth speech, and night unto night showeth knowledge" (Ps. 19:1, 2).

"In the beginning was the Word, and the Word was with God, and the Word was God . . . And the Word was made flesh, and dwelt among us (and we beheld his glory, the glory of the only begotten of the Father,) full of grace and truth" (John 1:1,14).

"That which was from the beginning, which we have heard, which we have seen with our eyes, which we have looked upon, and our hands have handled, of the Word of life; (For the life was manifested, and we have seen it, and bear witness, and show unto you eternal life, which was with the Father, and was manifested unto us;) That which we have seen and heard declare we unto you . . . " (I John 1:1-3).

"Do we begin again to commend ourselves? or need we, as some others, epistles of commendation to you, or letters of commendation from you? Ye are our epistles written in our hearts, known and read of all men: Forasmuch as ye are manifestly declared to be the epistles of Christ ministered by us, written not with ink, but with the Spirit of the living God; not in tables of stone, but in fleshy tables of the heart" (II Cor. 3:1-3).

"Hold fast the form of sound words, which thou hast heard of me, in faith and love which is in Christ Jesus" (II Tim. 1:13).

"Holding fast the faithful word as he hath been taught, that he may be able by sound doctrine both to exhort and to convince the gainsayers" (Titus 1:9).

"For the word of God is quick, and powerful, and sharper than any twoedged sword, piercing even to the dividing asunder of soul and spirit, and of the joints and marrow, and is a discerner of the thoughts and intents of the heart"(Heb. 4:12).

"It is the spirit that quickeneth; the flesh profiteth nothing; the words that I speak unto you, they are spirit, and they are life" (John 6:63).

WHAT DO YOU SAY?

1. What new elements in our culture demand a new look at our approach to communicating the gospel?

2. What elements of our traditional means of transmitting the gospel no longer get through to modern man? How can these be changed?

3. What aspects of present day church worship services fail to communicate to contemporary man? What can the church do to improve its presentation of the gospel?

4. If the content of the gospel is unchanging and eternal, how better can it be presented to meet the needs of our changing world?

5. If the medium really is an integral part of the message, how does this affect the manner in which the gospel is presented?

6. What is the place of the Bible in a world of electronic circuitry? Could electronics make the printed Bible obsolete? Why or why not?

7. How should Christians adopt their strategy to the electronic communications explosion? What are the implications of instant global communication through satellites?

8. McLuhan's theses make the power or effectiveness of the message relative to the media used to present it. Is this a valid assumption? Does this contradict Biblical teaching? How?

9. Are there any basic dangers in McLuhan's ideas? What assumptions could be misleading? Do his assumptions go too far?

10. What are the implications of John 1:1 in the light of McLuhan's emphasis that the medium is the message?

11. Jesus said, ". . . the words I speak to you, they are spirit, they are life." In the light of McLuhan's theses how could you interpret these words?

12. How does McLuhan's emphasis affect the ministry of the pastor? The missionary?

13. If the effective communication of the gospel is so closely related to the medium or the messenger, what should a Christian's goal be in order to effectively present the gospel?

14. If being literate in today's world means being more than well read and exposed to all the media, what changes would need to take place in the average church's approach to Christian education?

Notes

1. *Interaction Magazine,* copyright Concordia Publishing House, October, 1968. Used by permission.

2. Copyright *Eternity Magazine,* October, 1967. Used by permission.

3. *Ibid.*

4. *Ibid.*

Is It Ever Right to Break a Law? 7

MANY CHRISTIANS TODAY deplore the exhibitions of social disorder prevalent in our society. Certainly much of what passes for valid protest and dissent comes too close to anarchy for approval. Yet the issues regarding civil disobedience are not as cut and dried as some Christians make them out to be.

Perhaps the basic problem stems from a failure to distinguish between protest against unjust laws in themselves (as those actions during the early civil rights movement), and demonstrations deliberately designed to break valid laws in the name of some "higher" cause (as disrupting traffic or destroying public property in protest against the Vietnam war). Most right thinking people deplore violent actions against society aimed at disrupting the life of a community. Yet is there not a valid form of protest (civil disobedience) that Christians can condone and even at times use themselves against laws that deny fundamental human rights and justice?

In 1963, Martin Luther King engaged in sit-ins, boycotts, and demonstrations for civil justice for Negroes in Birmingham, Alabama. Dr. King and his followers met stiff resistance from Bull Connor, the commissioner of public safety, who sought to use every means possible to stop Dr. King from achieving equality for the Negroes in Birmingham. The most potent means available to Connor was the "law." Therefore when the Christian Southern Leadership Conference sought to dramatize the inferior status of the Negro in the South by a march to the city hall of Birmingham, Bull Connor resisted not only with violence but by the very means of the law. He obtained a court order that the SCLC cease their activities. By this legal maneuver their efforts could be effectively stopped by delaying court action until the momentum of the civil rights cause disappeared.

After much agony of soul, SCLC leaders decided to disobey the court injunction on the basis that those who would not obey a law of the Supreme Court, could not justly demand obedience to their own laws. There was a higher law to be obeyed that could not in good conscience be ignored.

Martin Luther King said in his famous, *Letter from Birmingham Jail,* ". . . there are two types of laws. One has not only legal but a moral responsibility to obey just laws. Conversely one has a moral responsibility to disobey unjust laws. I would agree with St. Augustine that 'an unjust law is no law at all.'

"In no sense do I advocate evading or defying the law, as would the rabid segregationist. That would lead to anarchy. One who breaks an unjust law must do so openly, lovingly and with a willingness to accept the penalty. I submit that an individual who breaks a law that conscience tells him is unjust, and who willingly accepts the penalty of imprisonment in order to arouse the conscience of his community over its injustice, is in reality expressing the highest respect for law."[1]

Civil disobedience, whatever its motivation, does not grant immunity for violation of the law.

Physical attacks against the police, assaults on private citizens who support an opposing idea, destroying public property in protest for one cause or another, is not civil disobedience in the classical sense of the term. Those who engage in defiant lawlessness should be judged by those laws set up for the protection of the citizenry.

Some Christians believe that to practice or condone civil disobedience is to loose a tiger of destruction. The welfare of a nation depends on law and order; lawlessness of any kind can only endanger the life of a nation. Therefore the only way to change inadequate or unjust laws is through the courts and the polls, not in the streets.

But what does a Christian do when a law becomes a tool of tyranny? What does the Christian do when law and order is merely a way of maintaining the status quo toward human rights for a minority group such as the Negro? Should Christians support such laws? Or should they openly violate them and demonstrate to build up public reaction against them?

As Henry David Thoreau asked, "Unjust laws exist, shall we be content to obey them or shall we endeavor to amend them at once?" The New Testament isn't exactly silent on this issue. Perhaps the actions of the apostles have something to say to us.

WHAT DOES THE BIBLE SAY?

In Acts 4 Peter and John preached the gospel. Many believed after the lame man was healed. They were brought before the religious leaders who threatened them if they continued to preach in the name of Jesus. How did they respond?

"And they called them, and commanded them

not to speak at all nor teach in the name of Jesus. But Peter and John answered and said unto them, Whether it be right in the sight of God to hearken unto you more than unto God, judge ye. For we cannot but speak the things which we have seen and heard. And now, Lord, behold their threatenings: and grant unto thy servants, that with all boldness they may speak thy word" (Acts 4:18-20, 29).

Again, in Acts 5 we have another account of the apostles boldly proclaiming the gospel. They were put into prison, serving the consequences of disobeying the set law of the day. The angel of the Lord sprung them out of the prison and they went right back to preaching — in disobedience to the order.

"And when they had brought them, they set them before the council; and the high priest asked them, Saying, Did not we straightly command you that ye should not teach in this name? and, behold, ye have filled Jerusalem with your doctrine, and intend to bring this man's blood upon us. Then Peter and the other apostle answered and said, We ought to obey God rather than men." (Acts 5:27-29).

"And the king of Egypt spake to the Hebrew midwives . . . and he said, When ye do the office of a midwife to the Hebrew women, and see them upon the stools; if it be a son, then ye shall kill him; but if it be a daughter, then she shall live. But the midwives feared God, and did not as the king of Egypt commanded them, but saved the men children alive" (Exod. 1:15-17).

"Thou, O king, hast made a decree, that

every man . . . shall fall down and worship the golden image: And whoso falleth not down and worshippeth, then he should be cast into the midst of a burning fiery furnace. There are certain Jews whom thou hast set over the affairs of the province of Babylon, Shadrach, Meshach, and Abednego; these men, O king, have not regarded thee: they serve not the gods, nor worship the golden image which thou hast set up. . . . Then they brought these men before the king. Nebuchadnezzar spake and said unto them, Is it true, O Shadrach, Meschach, and Abednego, do not ye serve my gods, nor worship the golden image which I have set up . . . Snadrach, Meshach, and Abednego, answered and said unto the king, O Nebuchadnezzar, we are not careful to answer thee in this matter. If it be so, our God whom we serve is able to deliver us from the burning fiery furnace and he will deliver us out of thy hand, O king. But if not, be it known unto thee, O king, that we will not serve thy gods, nor worship the golden image which thou hast set up" (Dan. 3:10-18).

". . . We shall not find any occasion against this Daniel, except we find it against him concerning the law of his God . . . All the presidents of the kingdom, the governors, and the princes, the counsellors, and the captains, have consulted together to establish a royal statute, and to make a firm decree, that whosoever shall ask a petition of any God or man for thirty days, save of thee, O king, he shall be cast into the den of lions . . . Now when Daniel knew that the writing was signed, he went into his house; and his windows being open in his chamber toward Jerusalem, he kneeled down upon his knees three times a day, and prayed, and gave thanks before his God, as he did aforetime. . . . they brought Daniel, and cast him into the den of lions. . . . My God hath sent his angel, and hath shut the lions' mouths, that they have not hurt me. . ." (Dan. 6:5-22).

The Bible also has much to say about being obedient to the laws of the land. Without this compliance the world would be in complete confusion. Anarchy would reign.

"Then saith he unto them, Render therefore unto Caesar the things that are Caesar's; and unto God the things that are God's (Matt. 22:21).

"Submit yourselves to every ordinance of man for the Lord's sake: whether it be to the king, as supreme; or unto governors, as unto them that are sent by him for the punishment of evildoers, and for the praise of them that do well. For so is the will of God, that with well doing you may put to silence the ignorance of foolish men" (I Peter 2:13-15).

"Put them in mind to be subject to principalities and powers, to obey magistrates, to be ready to every good work" (Titus 3:1).

"Let every soul be subject unto the higher powers. For there is no power but of God: the powers that be are ordained of God. Whosoever therefore resisteth the power, resisteth the ordinance of God: and they that resist shall receive to themselves damnation. For rulers are not a terror to good works, but to the evil. Wilt thou then not be afraid of the power? do that which is good, and thou shalt have praise of the same: For he is the minister of God to thee for good. But if thou do that which is evil, be afraid; for he beareth not the sword in vain: for he is the minister of God, a revenger to execute wrath upon him that doeth evil. Wherefore ye must needs be subject, not only for wrath, but also for conscience sake. For this cause pay ye tribute also: for they are God's ministers, attending continually upon this very thing. Render therefore to all their dues: tribute to whom tribute is due; custom to whom custom; fear to whom fear; honor to whom honor" (Rom. 13:1-7).

WHAT DO YOU SAY?

1. Since we have some clear-cut examples of civil disobedience in the Scriptures, should this be an accepted Christian approach to changing unjust situations?

2. Is there any difference in the fact that the orders to desist in Acts 4 and 5 came from religious leaders rather than from civil leaders? Did the religious leaders have civil authority?

3. Are the principles of Jesus' refusal to follow Sabbath laws a form of civil disobedience?

4. The situations in Daniel 4 and 6 are definite acts of civil disobedience. Would we condemn the four Hebrews for this? Could they have taken any alternate position? Are there any situations in which one can do nothing but disobey a law?

5. In what ways does Peter seem to contradict himself in the statements in I Peter 2 as compared

to his actions in Acts 4 and 5? How do you reconcile this apparent contradiction?

6. Is there a difference between protest demonstrations and civil disobedience? Could the public demonstration be a proper means of Christian protest? Is civil disobedience a proper form of dissent?

7. If a local government passed a law prohibiting door-to-door visitation on grounds that it was an invasion of privacy, would you insist that your church desist in its visitation programs? How would you test the validity of this law? And if it was proven constitutional, would you obey it?

8. If a law was passed prohibiting the distribution of religious literature to other than church adherents, would you obey or disobey that law?

9. Is it simply right to obey laws that fit into our ideas of personal or group liberties and to disobey or circumvent those laws that interfere with our plans?

10. Does the form of government under which the Christian lives determine what is allowable civil disobedience and whether it is right to so act? Since civil disobedience is permitted in the United States, but not in Russia, is it right where it is permitted and wrong where it is not?

Notes

1. In "Letter from Birmingham Jail," *Why We Can't Wait*. Copyright 1963 by Harper and Row, Publishers. Used by permission.

Is Modern Technology a Threat to Christianity?

IN ONE WAY OR ANOTHER modern technology affects the lives of most people in the world. The rise of the electronic computer is beginning to change the very fabric of society. Many people are still unsure of the computer. Is it friend or foe? Will it cause unending unemployment or replace the function of the human brain? The uninitiated wonder whether computers will be developed with the ability to think for themselves.

Computers, and the electronic technology that we call automation, have made deep inroads into our society and promise changes beyond our imagination. The growth of our technology and automation has been phenomenal in the last twenty years. It is estimated that by 1970 computers will be a $22 billion business. (In 1965 $6 billion worth of computers were in use).

Computers are at work in business computing complex financial problems, forecasting sales, determining markets and checking almost everyone's credit. The medical profession is using computers to aid in diagnosing a patient's illness and prescribing remedies.

Modern food processing is fast becoming automated. Farming is becoming one of the most automated industries. The phenomenal advances in space exploration and flights to the moon would have been totally impossible without the accurate and speedy computations of computers. Space explorations like the Apollo series are dependent primarily on computers to make the precise calculations needed to travel in space. Computers are able to make millions of calculations a second — a feat that would be impossible for multitudes of men to accomplish in weeks.

The advances of modern technology stagger the mind. Some scientists look forward to the day when man will perfect computers that will reproduce replicas of themselves. Scientists predict that through a combination of biology and electronics — "bionics" — such a feat is in the realm of possibility. The prospects of greater breakthroughs in scientific know-how to benefit mankind through applied technology are unimaginable. The late President John F. Kennedy said, "As we begin to master the potentialities of modern science we move toward a new era in which science can fulfill its creative promise and help bring into existence the happiest society the world has ever known."

Modern technological advance — staggering as it is — has clouded man's thinking on basic issues of existence. Those matters that humanize and personalize man, such as human concerns for one another, mercy, love, and compassion, take a back seat to the pursuit of better things and faster methods and machines. Americans and other nations have substituted a confidence in a technology for a dependence upon God. Technology has become the ultimate cure for all ills. One writer has characterized American technology as its theology that promises salvation by material works.

Yet looming over all the good and progress we have received from modern technology, there is the haunting fear that it is pushing man toward the worst even while bringing him to a utopia of better living. Two questions rise in men's minds about the result of this technological revolution: What is man becoming? and What will become of man?

The first question concerns the influence of modern technology on man psychologically, morally, and socially. Is modern man in danger of becoming depersonalized to such a degree that he amounts to nothing more than a controllable robot? Will man become a servant of the very technology he has created? Will the fears, unrest, and inevitable change in a highly technological society breed a humanity controlled by pills, the formulas of which were created by a computer? Will a new generation, largely taught by teaching machines rather than people, shake off all respect for accepted traditions and moral standards? Will despotic control be made easier when men's minds are conditioned by global communication networks?

The second question asks: What will become of man? The question concerns itself with man's future and his existence on this planet. Major world powers now have the ability to destroy one another and most of the rest of the world. All this is possible through man's scientific accomplishments. It is technologically possible now to destroy the world. With no sign that the nations of the world are willing to disarm, this is frightening. The secrets of the atomic and hydrogen bomb are getting in the hands of more and more nations of the world, most of whom have the technology to deliver such bombs around the world. What will become of man? Will he reduce his state to primitive times by a major halocaust? Will he so threaten himself by increasing the means of destroying himself to the point where all the world stands on edge in fear of an indiscriminate push of a button?

No matter which of these two questions we consider, they both point us to significant problems of modern life, the problems of really knowing who we are and what is our destiny. Modern technology forces us to ask in a different sense the question the psalmist posed: "What is man that thou art mindful of him?" What is man's place in the world? What is his place in history? What is his mission?

Myron R. Chartier said in *Christianity Today*, "Science has given man the objective method and man has been able to assert his power and authority over the materials of his world. The mountains have yielded their iron, gold, and uranium. The power of water has been harnessed. The oceans have been imprisoned within the lines of latitude and longitude, and the wonder of air has been captured by the isobars of the meteorologist. Man is the undisputed ruler of his world.

"But this same tool with which he has split the atom and invaded space is also the weapon that threatens man himself. For he is part of the world he seeks to dominate. The empirical process by which he elevated himself to the position of lord of the whole earth informs him that he is merely a temporary chemical episode in the life of one of the minor planets. Man has organized his world into categories of thingness so he can force it to serve his imaginative desires, but in the process he has discovered that he himself is a thing. The king on the throne of the universe finds himself just another statistic."[1]

Modern technology has excelled in the application of scientific principles to control of the material resources of our civilization. Because of the tremendous success in control of these material aspects of our culture, man has become dependent upon them and in fact welded to them.

In doing so he has excluded from his thinking any necessity for dependence upon a supernatural intrusion into his world. For many, the existence of God is no longer a live issue since man is quite able to get along by himself. Human ingenuity and applied technology will enable man to solve the problems "God" did not solve since the world began. Hunger, sickness, death — someday science will have the answers. Man has come of age!

The crucial question, however, is whether man really has come of age? Is he still like a little boy playing with matches? Is technological efficiency synonymous with moral or spiritual maturity? Can man really go it alone?

Some Christians doubt very much that modern man has really attained a utopian world. Carl Henry says: "The crucial issue for modern man, I think, is whether he will recognize that his creatureliness and his sinfulness place limits on the fulfillment of human aspirations, and that the abundant life simply can't be found in an abundance of material things and in an abundance of sex, or in an abundance of status, or in an abundance of leisure, if we come to the leisure era. Christ's word is, I think, still the most relevant counsel to the current age: 'Seek first the Kingdom of God, and all desirable things will come as by-products.' Improved material conditions don't overcome man's softness of his moral delusion or corruption. I think there are more wonderful possibilities that can be held out for modern man even than creating parts for wornout bodies, magnificent as that is, or regulating human fertility, or communicating by satellite, or living on artificial food. God can turn sinners into new creatures. And He will raise the dead. And we can enter into our closet and talk to the eternal Spirit. And we can enjoy meat to eat that others cannot see. There's a city more durable than the secular city — the New Jerusalem — and in it death will be abolished. I think that if modern man devoted half as much interest to the spiritual and moral world as he does to technological efficiency, there would be a staggering religious awakening and a regaining of eternal truth that would make contemporary technology rather than theology seem to rest on a plateau."[2]

WHAT DOES THE BIBLE SAY?

Since the Bible was written in nontechnological eras, it might seem logical to conclude that it has nothing to say to a technological age. On the contrary, its emphasis on the spiritual nature of the Christian life and conflict, and the presentation of God's personal concern about humanity have much to say to our generation. What a contrast between the personal interest God shows in His children and the growing impersonalization of humanity as it seeks to control itself through technological advancement.

"His going forth is from the end of the heaven, and his circuit into the ends of it: and there is nothing hid from the heat thereof. The law of the Lord is perfect, converting the soul: the testimony of the Lord is sure, making wise the simple. The statutes of the Lord are right, rejoicing the heart: the commandment of the Lord is pure, enlightening the eyes. The fear of the Lord is clean, enduring forever: the judgments of the Lord are true and righteous altogether. More to be desired are they than gold, yea, than much fine gold: sweeter also than honey and the honeycomb" (Ps. 19:6-10).

"I am come that they might have life, and that they might have it more abundantly" (John 10:10).

"For in him dwelleth all the fullness of the Godhead bodily. And ye are complete in him, which is the head of all principality and power"(Col. 2:9-10).

"For though we walk in the flesh, we do not war after the flesh: (For the weapons of our warfare are not carnal, but mighty through God to the pulling down of strongholds;) Casting down imaginations, and every high thing that exalteth itself against the knowledge of God, and bringing into captivity every thought to the obedience of Christ" (II Cor. 10:3-5).

"But he anwered and said, it is written, Man shall not live by bread alone, but by every word that proceedeth out of the mouth of God" (Matt. 4:4).

"But seek ye first the kingdom of God, and his righteousness; and all these things shall be added unto you" (Matt. 6:33).

WHAT DO YOU SAY?

1. In what ways is modern man losing his freedom as technology becomes more and more a factor in daily living?

2. What tendencies do dependence on machines produce in man?

3. To what is modern technology leading man? Name the good things as well as the undesireable.

4. Technology tends to impersonalize man. How does this conflict with Christian beliefs about the worth of a person?

5. Science and technology have done wonders for mankind. What attitudes should the Christian have toward modern scientific advancements?

6. What are some of the dangers of putting too much faith in science?

7. Is there anything in the human personality that will prevent man from becoming a slave to the machines he invents?

8. How do you explain man's willingness to accept science and technology with little or no questioning?

9. What is the difference in the abundant life provided by modern science and that which is promised in John 10:10? Is there any harmony in these two concepts?

10. What can the church do to maintain its stature as a spiritual force in this materialistic age?

Notes

1. Myron R. Chartier, "Depersonalization and Resurrection Faith." Copyright © *Christianity Today*, April 12, 1968. Reprinted by permission.

2. Carl F. Henry, "Technology, Modern Man, and the Gospel." Copyright © *Christianity Today*, July 5, 1968. Reprinted by permission.

How Much Clothing Can We Take Off? 9

A SIXTH GRADE CLASS took an educational trip to a local art gallery. At the end of the tour they had to pass through a section of paintings of nude women. The boys snickered; the girls were embarrassed. Later, when some of the parents complained to the teacher that she should have had better judgment than to take the children through that section, she defended the action by saying that they had to learn about nudity sooner or later.

A television station in Chicago cut some scenes from a film before it was put on the air. Critics told the manager that such action was unnecessary because the "adult" audience wanted to see the nude scenes. In fact, many assured the station manager that nudity would soon be common fare for television watchers.

Recently in Africa, the Tanzanian government ordered 100,000 Masai tribespeople to put on shorts and trousers. One Masai leader responded by saying, "If God made Adam and Eve nude, why do we have to go against what God originally intended?"

It seems that most risqué magazines and paperback books have won acceptance by the American public. No longer are there strong compaigns to get such magazines with full page and foldout pages of nudes banned from newsstands. Even some of the general interest magazines are beginning to offer articles accompanied by illustrations that suggest, "Take it off, take it all off!" The cult of nudity has influenced much of our society. And while the nude form isn't yet generally accepted by the public, semi-nudity seems to have widespread acceptance, especially in fashions. This forces Christians to ask the question, "How much clothing can we take off?"

Examining the field of fashions, we find that our Western culture places great emphasis on styles. Eastern cultures, unless they have been influenced by the West, have had little change in their clothing fashions over the centuries. An excellent example of the unchangeableness of styles is found in Arab clothing.

Several things have influenced the changes of styles in America. The coming of the Industrial Revolution made mass production possible so clothing items were made less expensively, and more than one style was available. Mass communications have accelerated the demands for new styles. Advertising has also played a large part in the constant change of our dress. By creating a new desire for new styles, advertising has often been the leader in change.

Betty Nohl, writing in *Interaction Magazine* pointed out that "at one time fashion helped establish a definite distinction between the classes. In the past a person's everyday dress reflected not only his occupation but even his morals. It hasn't been too long since dyed hair, cosmetics, black stockings, and a twirling purse were the unmistakable trademark of 'that kind of woman' . . . Now fashion is everybody's game, and the game has no rules.

"Even the adjectives describing fashions have changed. Once clothes were soft and lovely, delicious and feminine, frilly and frothy, clinging and delicate. Today they are smashing, bold, aggressive, irreverent, wild, vibrant, jungle-hued, eye-popping, free-wheeling, socko!

"So fashion in the sixties not only changes: it also generates controversy."[1]

Fashions continue to change because humans have a love to decorate their bodies. They find that their clothing can be a means of expressing their personality. Clothing can give status and add to sexual attractiveness. This is especially true for the female.

When we begin to talk about modesty to the younger generation, we only draw blank stares. They don't know what we are talking about. Besides, since many of them have lived most of their teen years in the era of the miniskirt and tight trousers, they do not look upon such clothing from the same point of view as do adults. They do not attach a moral implication to the shortness of a skirt or the tightness of slacks just below the hip line. Many Christian youths cannot fathom how adults can attach any spiritual significance to whether a hemline is three or four inches above the knee. It isn't the length of a skirt that makes one spiritual, they loudly proclaim.

Betty Nohl states that "responsibility is the key-word in relation to modern fashions. People freed by God's love in Christ will be able to react to changing fashions with courage and keen judgment.

"They will be able to sense the pressure the fashion industry continually exerts on them and to *live* with it.

"They will be able to resist the lure of soft

79

words urging them to buy this or use that, to wear this or try that, when they don't need it.

"They will be interested in fashion but not obsessed by it; they will know that wearing the latest cannot guarantee happiness, popularity, or love.

"They will be able to take fashion or leave it. They will not be overwhelmed by the need to conform. They will realize they can still be "in" with God when they choose to be "out" so far as certain fashions are concerned.

"Young people will be able to subject passing fashions to a secure faith, confident that God's grace supplies a beauty far exceeding that of even the most stylish modes of modern dress.

"And so, as in all our teaching, we seek to help youth assimilate fashions in their total perspective as Christian people. And we trust that the Spirit is at work with them, filling young hearts with a desire for standards whose measure is always the Christ who gave His life that we might have joy and life forever."[2]

But since many fashions are derived from a desire to live in the nude or semi-nude state, or to use the semi-nude state to attract the opposite sex, we must consider the Christian attitudes toward nudity.

Gordon Jaeck, M.A., ACSW, of Wheaton College, contributing to an article titled "The New Nudity" in *Christian Life* magazine, wrote, "Nudity is not wrong in itself, rather the use to which it is put determines its rightness or wrongness. The artist asserts that the nude is an art object and, therefore, completely neutral. On the other hand, nudity can be used to attract or stimulate, depending on the use of clothing, the pose, etc. In some cases it can become obscene.

"Secondly, there are many good aspects to the American moral revolution . . . The contemporary openness concerning sex, the use of marriage counseling to solve sexual problems and the aggressiveness and creativity of young people who are seeking answers to an honest effort to develop an integrated approach to life — these reflect changing sexual attitudes moving in a positive direction.

"A third principle is that there appears to be a parallel between today's emphasis on psychological unmasking, equated with openness and honesty, and physical unmasking or nakedness. Both imply accepting ourself, including our physical body, in a realistic and healthy way.

"While various forms of nudity have been common in other cultures and eras, one of its unique characteristics in contemporary society represents a kind of search for identity. It may well be a revolt against the increasing anonymity of American society."[3]

Jaeck goes on to state some ways in which the Church and the individual Christian can help make this moral revolution beneficial to our society. In answer to the question, "What should the individual Christian's attitude be?" he answers:

"As Christians and as a church we must rethink our relationship to American society. Perhaps our greatest contribution would be to reenter the world.

"There is a need for the individual Christian to establish a personal, rational and 'Christian' position in the matter of public nudity. Censorship begins at the individual level. We can choose what we read, what we view on TV or screen.

"Thirdly, I would see professionally competent

sex education as a basic responsibility of Christian parents."[4]

In the same article, Eugene Johnson, chairman of the art department at Bethel College, St. Paul, Minnesota, states that "a distinction, however, ought to be made as to the manner in which the artist may use the human form. There is a difference between the 'nude' and 'nudity.' Nudity implies nakedness, to be aware of the absence of clothes. It either arouses embarrassment and shame or exhibitionism and sexual self-consciousness. The nude figure may be quite neutral when the human form is used as an esthetic vehicle to express rhythm, motion, balance or symbol. 'Nudity' is concerned with desire, the nude with design."[5]

WHAT DOES THE BIBLE SAY?

"And the eyes of them both were opened, and they knew that they were naked and they sewed fig leaves together, and made themselves aprons" (Gen. 3:7).

"Unto Adam also and to his wife did the Lord God make coats of skins, and clothed them" (Gen 3:21).

"Wherefore, if God so clothe the grass of the field, which today is, and tomorrow is cast into the oven, shall he not much more clothe you, O ye of little faith? Therefore take no thought, saying, What shall we eat? or, What shall we drink: or, Wherewithal shall we be clothed" (Matt. 6:30 31).

"Who can find a virtuous woman? . . . for all her household are clothed with scarlet" (Prov. 31:10, 21).

"Thou shalt not wear a garment of divers sorts, as of woolen and linen together" (Deut. 22:11).

"In like manner also, that women adorn themselves in modest apparel, with shamefacedness and sobriety; not with braided hair, or gold, or pearls, or costly array" (I Tim. 2:9).

WHAT DO YOU SAY?

1. How does the Christian establish a code of modesty when fashions are constantly changing? Are there any rigid rules that we can establish? Why or why not?

2. Do we have any scriptural guidelines to use in the matters of selecting clothing? How would you apply Deuteronomy 22:11 to this? How does Paul's sensitivity to his own actions relating to their effect on others' behavior (cf. I Cor. 6:12; I Cor. 10:23, 32; Rom. 14:21) relate to a Christian's approach to dress?

3. Is it more Christian simply to be five to ten years behind the times in matters of style and dress? If not, why aren't more Christians in leadership in the fashion world?

4. Why do so many evangelicals condemn young people for their fashions? Why do we often equate clothing to morality?

5. Is it wrong in one culture to wear little or no clothing and right in another culture? Why?

6. If the matter of clothing is simply a cultural thing, how can the Christian establish any absolutes concerning rules that govern what we shall wear? How does Paul's emphasis on the sanctity of the body (I Cor. 3:16, 17; I Cor. 6:19, 20)

relate to the question of what clothes Christians wear?

7. Why couldn't we simply legislate the matter — like the Australians, who in December 1968 passed a law stating that bikinis must measure 2" at the hip? Couldn't we simply legislate that all clothing meet certain specifications as to the amount of the body that should be covered?

8. If from the Christian viewpoint nudity is wrong in our culture, what can we do to reverse the present trends to "take it all off"? The Old Testament seems to treat exposure of the human body as sinful (cf. Gen. 9:20-27; Lev. 18:6-19; 20:17-21;) What relevance does this have to the question of nudity today?

9. What can we do to help teens establish a code of modesty and still keep up with the latest fashions?

10. If we paid less attention to nudity, would the present fad soon fade?

Notes

1. *Interaction Magazine,* copyright Concordia Publishing House, October 1968, p. 9. Used by permission.

2. *Ibid.,* p. 11.

3. *Christian Life Magazine,* copyright © November, 1968, p. 47. Used by permission of Christian Life Publications, Inc., Gundersen Drive and Schmale Road, Wheaton, Ill. 60187.

4. *Ibid.*

5. *Ibid.*

Does the Christian Have Any Problems in Today's Business World? 10

A LEWIS HARRIS SURVEY, based upon 2,000 interviewee reactions, revealed that 42% of the people thought that most businessmen would do anything, honest or otherwise, to make a buck; 77% regarded business as a "dog-eat-dog" affair.

Nation's Business magazine reported that college students have even less favorable opinions. They have extremely low opinions of the ethical practices of businessmen. Most feel that the businessman's primary concern is to "make money, more money, much money — by any means possible."

Unscrupulous businessmen seem to be as American as apple pie. And even some Christian businessmen have poor reputations. We've all had some unfortunate dealings with unethical business people.

Business ethics is a complicated problem. The many-faceted responsibilities of a businessman cloud his ethical considerations. He must keep his stockholders satisfied or he will not have sufficient funds to operate the business. He must satisfy his workers or they will not produce at an efficient rate. He must produce goods or services at a price acceptable to consumers, being constantly aware of competitors.

The temptation to make a fast buck plagues every businessman. Possibly he has struggled for many years in his "honesty is the best policy" approach. Possibly he has eked out only a modest living. Suddenly an opportunity comes to make a sizeable profit, a once-in-a-lifetime experience. It will bring in outstanding returns if there is a slight shifting of expense figures or a slight lessening of quality — something that possibly no one will ever detect. A slight change in the specifications would save him considerable expense, thus adding to the profits. Why not this once?

Of course, all choices aren't this clearcut. Sometimes they involve a stroke of genius; sometime they are made complex by the unavoidability of possible alternatives or possible outcomes. A further complication: God never dictates our actions but gives us a series of ground rules that permit us considerable freedom of choice. We can choose to be unethical.

Too often Christian businessmen think the Charles Sheldon (*In His Steps*) approach easily solves everything. Simply ask, "What would Jesus do?" But inadequate information or various alternatives hinder the businessman from knowing which course even the Lord would take. William A. Spurrier, in his book, *Ethics and Business*, says that the Christian is called upon to take Christ's perfect love and apply it to imperfect situations. Unfortunately the Christian doesn't possess this quality of love nor has he attained perfect motivation for all his acts.

Applying the Ten Commandments or the Golden Rule or maintaining a Sunday ethic are applicable to everyday business affairs. But the Bible doesn't spell out every business principle. Simple moral or Bible verse answers for every problem in life do not exist. To believe such, one must be incredibly naive. This is especially true in business because the businessman must contend with many opposing forces: management–labor; profit–wages; quality–cleaply-priced products. Moral choices are complicated by the unavailability of facts about possible alternatives and possible outcomes. God does not zero in to dictate the actions of a Christian businessman. Rather, He gives us ground rules and the freedom to apply them in relationships to the best of our knowledge and business acumen.

In an article on "Business Ethics and the Christian" in the November, 1965 *Lutheran Witness,* John M. Hess, associate professor of marketing at the University of Colorado, says, "I believe man's ability to act ethically can, like faith, grow by seeking God's assistance and guidance and by utilizing our God-given intelligence to approach each ethical dilemma in a Christian manner.

"By systematically approaching business situations in a highly conscious manner, man can at least improve his performance. The following 7-point approach is an attempt to aid the Christian in meeting business situations ethically:

1. Determine his responsibility to the other individuals involved and to God.

2. Develop a relevant personal code of ethics based on Scripture.

3. Attempt to reflect this code in all his actions and revise it as God blesses him with additional spiritual maturity.

4. Always be alert to recognize possible ethical implications in all decisions or actions.

5. Seek outside assistance in recognizing the moral way. Turn to God in prayer and to clergymen and fellow Christians for advice.

6. Decide the moral action.

7. Take that action.

"The actual decision sequence may be said to have three steps: (1) recognizing the problem, (2) recognizing the moral way of handling it, and (3) making the moral choice.

"Undesirable behavior can be the outcome of failure at any of the three steps — failure to recognize the problem, failure to diagnose it correctly and to recognize the moral route; or failure to take the moral action even though one knows what it is. As ultimately judged, every business decision is an individual one for which the decision-maker must take personal responsibility."[1]

In the same issue, Wilmar F. Bernthal, professor of management at Colorado, gives the following statements to help employers act ethically toward employees:

"There are some ways in which the employer can, if he wishes, exercise Christian responsibility toward employees in making employment decisions.

1. He can keep employees well-informed of impending changes so that they can prepare themselves for the new demands which may be made on them and for the new opportunities which may come their way.

2. He can use his knowledge and influence to provide education and training opportunities to those employees who are willing and able to take advantage of them, and to help find employment opportunities elsewhere for those facing dismissal.

3. He can assure that the transition to automation is made with justice and equity for those affected. This may involve giving them a voice in the process of making changes by providing means for regular consultation, often through collective bargaining, rather than by imposing new methods through unilateral action.

"The ultimate test of whether an act is ethical in the Christian sense is not the act itself but whether the motive which prompts the act is one of Christian love.

"While a businessman may be acting ethically in dismissing an employee for economic reasons, his calling as a Christian constrains him also, by the love of Christ, to help those in need."[2]

The Royal Bank of Canada Monthly Letter for September, 1964, had these comments on "Self-regulation in Business":

"Men cannot be closely associated in business without a clashing of self-interest which gives rise to ethical problems. We occasionally run into the sinister doctrine of expediency, which sanctions such antisocial slogans as "might is right," and some rules are needed.

"The word 'ethics' may repel some people because they think of it as somehow applying to their religion and without a place in the hurly-burly of business life.

"Ethics covers what has been found satisfactory in a way of doing business. It involves not only acts which are covered by the legal code but acts that are in the shadow land of unenforceable well-doing. It codifies in an outward way the inward sensation of rightness we feel about our contacts and dealings with other human beings ...

"The practicality of business ethics is illustrated in an earthy way by Harry Emerson Fosdick, author of *On Being a Real Person*, in his lecture 'Six Ways to Tell Right from Wrong': The test of common sense — should I say to myself, 'Don't be silly!'? The test of sportsmanship — do I propose to abide by the rules of fair play? The test of our best selves — have I carried the decision up to my finest self: The test of publicity — what if every body knew what I am proposing to do? The test of our most admired personality — what would he do under the circumstances? The test of foresight — where is this course of behavior coming out? . . .

"Honesty in business may be actuated by policy, but that policy has come into good repute because many people believe it worthwhile. Just as soon as honesty is adopted for the sake of greater profits it mysteriously ceases to be honesty.

"Honesty is not the mere giving of the right change. In his *Offices*, Cicero outlined the notion of honesty under these heads: (1) Sagacious inquiry and observation for the finding out of truth; (2) Care to render to every man what is his due and to stand to one's words in all promises and bargains; (3) Keeping of our words and actions within due limits of order and decency.

"Perhaps the surest test of an individual's integrity is his refusal to do or say anything that would damage his self-respect. The cornerstone of his value system is the question "What will I think of myself if I do this?"

"There is a phrase which you come across in country districts in Ireland: 'So-and-so has a Word.' This adage 'A man's word is as good as his bond' has vital meaning in today's business life."[3]

WHAT DOES THE BIBLE SAY?

"He becometh poor that dealeth with a slack hand; but the hand of the diligent maketh rich" (Prov. 10:4).

"The hand of the diligent shall bear rule: but the slothful shall be under tribute" (Prov. 12:24).

"The slothful man roasteth not that which he

took in hunting; but the substance of a diligent man is precious" (Prov. 12:27).

"Seest thou a man diligent in his business? he shall stand before kings; he shall not stand before obscure men" (Prov. 22:29).

In the parable of the talents (Matt. 25:14-30) Jesus referred to the man who hid the money as a "wicked and slothful servant" (v. 26). This would imply that the way we invest our money has some moral overtones.

"Not slothful in business; fervent in spirit; serving the Lord . . . Recompense to no man evil for evil. Provide things honest in the sight of all men" (Rom. 12:11, 17).

"Providing for honest things, not only in the sight of the Lord, but also in the sight of men" (2 Cor. 8:21).

"Servants, obey in all things your masters according to the flesh; not with eyeservice, as menpleasers; but in singleness of heart, fearing God: And whatsoever ye do, do it heartily, as to the Lord, and not unto men" (Col. 3:22-23).

"And that ye study to be quiet, and to do your own business, and to work with your own hands, as we command you; That ye may walk honestly toward them that are without, and that ye may have lack of nothing" (I Thess. 4:11, 12).

"For even when we were with you, this we commanded you, that if any would not work, neither should he eat. For we hear that there are some which walk among you disorderly, working not at all, but are busybodies. Now them that are such we command and exhort by our Lord Jesus Christ, that with quietness they work, and eat their own bread. But ye, brethren, be not weary in well doing" (II Thess. 3:10-13).

"Let him that stole steal no more; but rather let him labor, working with his hands the thing which is good, that he may have to give to him that needeth" (Eph 4:28).

"Behold, the hire of the labourers who have reaped down your fields, which is of you kept by fraud, crieth: and the cries of them which have reaped are entered into the ears of the Lord of sabaoth" (James 5:4).

WHAT DO YOU SAY?

1. Is there such a thing as a Christian businessman or is this a misnomer? Should we simply say he is a Christian in business?

2. To what should a Christian attribute his business successes, to his faith or to business principles?

3. Are incompetent businessmen to be tolerated simply because they are Christians?

4. Is it better to act ethically and fail than to engage in any business that has questionable aspects even though it can be a good avenue for Christian witness?

5. Should Christian organizations assume the attitude that their employees are working for the Lord as well as for the company? Should a church-related organization's wage scale be comparable to secular organizations?

6. Does business ethics govern where a business-

man gets his supplies and materials as well as where and how he sells his products?

7. Is it ethical to advertise only some aspects of a product or service so that the public gets the impression that the product or company is the greatest ever?

8. What obligation does an employer have when a machine can take the place of a man in the company?

9. In our rapidly changing technology, is the employer ethically obligated to provide the employees job security, continued employment, or full retirement benefits?

10. If an employee doesn't give a full measure of work for his pay, is it ethical to accept a paycheck in full?

11. Is it ethical to favor some customers over others either because of friendships or because of the amount of business?

12. Is it ethical to take advantage of someone else's discount privileges?

13. Housewives engage in business in the supermarket. Is it ethical to squeeze and pick off bad grapes before weighing? Is it ethical for the supermarket manager to sell inferior or unusable merchandise?

Notes

1. Used by permission of the *Lutheran Witness*.

2. *Ibid.*

3. Used by permission of the Royal Bank of Canada.

11 | Is Church Music Obsolete?

THE APOSTLE PAUL exhorted believers to admonish one another in "psalms and hymns and spiritual songs" (Col. 3:16). The exact musical expression of these three types is not clear, but it is plain that Christians from the early days of the church have used various forms of music as an integral part of their worship experience. These forms have changed from century to century. Various periods of church history have produced different kinds of church music. Some periods emphasized congregational participation, others stressed choral or instrumental music with only limited congregational response.

From ancient times psalms were used as the accepted musical form for expressing praise and worship to God. The chant was a popular form before the Reformation and was possibly the form dating back to the Davidic time. Luther wrote hymns that could be used with the popular beer-house ballads of his time. With the coming of Isaac Watts and modern hymnody, psalms were paraphrased and given popular new tunes. Emphasis on chanting psalms diminished, and the era of Watts, Wesley, and other 18th-century hymn writers produced the great hymns that would predominate Protestant hymnology into the 20th century.

In the nineteenth century another style appeared — the gospel song. The gospel song took the emphasis off the more formal style of praise and worship and stressed the personal experience of the believer. They have often been labeled "I and Me" songs. The revival spirit of the late 19th and early 20th centuries produced a vast number of gospel songs which now dominate most non-liturgical Protestant hymnbooks. Interestingly, the gospel song style has dominated evangelical hymnbooks during most of the present century.

The various kinds of music produced and used in the periods of church history reflect the nature of their times. New forms and styles of music that have become popular in the history of the church have had their effect on Christian musical expression.

Today, the music that is popular in the secular world is having its effect on the development of new forms of sacred music. Like all innovations, such changes and experiments do not come without controversy and differences of opinion. Definite musical patterns and style have developed in our time, making many of the songs we sing sound obsolete, perhaps for no other reason than that they no longer speak to the needs of modern man.

Some hymns and gospel songs have qualities that make them significant and meaningful today. Others, perhaps because they reflected more of the character of their time than the eternal truths of Christ, are obsolete and without significance for men today. What was significant in the late 19th century may be merely sentimental today. Many feel that there is a definite need to communicate the gospel in a vital and living way to our generation through some kind of adaptation of modern musical styles.

Some have experimented with jazz, others have adapted modern folk music to express Christian truths and experience. Many Christians do not accept these modern forms as legitimate means to express sacred truths. Many are satisfied with the gospel songs they have repeated hundreds of times since they learned them in Sunday school. Any change comes close to a compromise with the devil.

There is by no means unanimity regarding what is suitable for Christian worship and what is not. Many who deplore modern jazz or folk music turned Christian would also condemn the more classical and liturgical sacred music as being too "high brow." Others would condemn all gospel songs and choruses as too naive and sentimental, preferring only chorales and stately hymns.

Some have pointed out that our unconcern and behind-the-times attitude can be seen by browsing through our commonly used hymnbooks. There is an extreme overbalance of hymns from the 18th and 19th centuries and a neglect of both music that preceded and succeeded that period.

"As a typical example, a popular worship hymnal published in this decade and used in many churches has not one hymn by a writer born in this century, and less than one percent of the writers are still living, with the youngest of these in his 70's."[1]

Christians, who have accepted an overabundance of new translations of the Bible, have been reluctant to give 20th-century songs and styles a place in their hymnology. Too few of our hymns reflect present day life and circumstances. Not that the old songs should all be scrapped, but perhaps they should be supplemented. Lawrence Richards asks, ". . . is it not sensible also to have in our worship books contemporary songs reflecting our lives today, with a message just as beautiful and even more relevant? Many of these songs already have been written and are on our sheet music and in our Sunday school song books. Can we find the courage to place them side by side with the hallowed hymns of a century ago? There is yet much more to be done as well. Where is the song that shows Christ with us downtown and not just *In the Garden*? Where is the song that reflects the presence and help of God in the often boring work of factory and not just while *We Plow the Fields, and Scatter*. Where is the song that indicates the Lord is with us in the roar of machines and not just when under the scorching sun and protected by the *Rock of Ages*. Can we produce and sing hymns that reflect us, our problems, concerns and goals, our needs, our circumstances, our lives — and show the risen and living Lord right there each step of the way?"[2]

Many evangelicals are not unaware of the pressures to do something about church music. They have heard of the "folk masses" and "sacred jazz" concerts, coffeehouse folk music and other experiments with modern forms. They are aware that some of our hymns and gospel songs have little meaning to modern youth and perhaps even had little to say to the former generations to which they were written.

For the most part new songs and styles have been presented as "specials" and have not become popular as congregational songs. Most of these songs have an immediate appeal to youth and are used primarily in youth meetings or at functions outside the church such as Young Life, Youth for Christ, and Campus Crusade rallies.

Evangelicals should put this situation in the perspective of the command to take the gospel to all the world. In other times, Christians had to adjust to new forms. Christians during the Reformation learned to accept Luther's transformed-from-the-beergarden tunes rather than listening to Gregorian chants. Staid Americans had to learn to sing gospel songs that sounded like Stephen Foster minstrels. Why can't Christians today learn to listen and use music taken from contemporary styles?

Don Hustad, former music teacher at Moody Bible Institute and organist for the Billy Graham Crusades, feels that Christians do not need to introduce jazz or ballet into churches, but do need to take advantage of their opportunities. He says, " . . . perhaps we should dare to capitalize on a popular folk-song style that is as harmless and pleasant as the art of Burl Ives or Peter, Paul and Mary — at least in our informal youth meetings or in evangelism among the surfing set.

"Many of us have decried the lack of fresh song expressing for our generation. Are the inheritors of the gospel song now too middle-class and reactionary to develop a truly new song for our day?

"Once again there should be a healthy, middle of the road course possible for the thinking believer. Such a viewpoint will not yield on the one hand to the temptation to close one's eyes to the necessity for making new judgments and evaluations in a safe, sterile obscurantism. But neither will it fall into the error of indiscriminate acceptance in a wild, destructive syncretism. Such a middle-of-the-roader should be far better equipped spiritually to find his way than the artist who bases judgments wholly on the shifting sands of 'aesthetic truth.' "[3]

Hustad is aware that, "time is a great sanctifier" and certain forms of music once held in disdain have become accepted art forms of music and used in Christian worship. He suggests, however, that certain popular forms of music taken from the world by the church had first become transformed and made fresh for the house of God. Artists, like Luther, removed the stench of the street and beergarden from the tunes before using them in Christian worship.

Music such as jazz, taken from the world, says Hustad, can be meaningful only if re-oriented biblically and theologically. It is not just a matter of transferring it from the night club to the church. Hustad says, "No doubt new musical styles will continue to emerge from the world of entertainment and find their way into the church. Jazz may well be one of them. But, as in all past days, if they do, it will be the result of clear musical workmanship, sound biblical and theological understanding and compelling Christian purpose."[4]

Perhaps it is too early to make such a judgment about rock and roll. After all it is still finding its way in the world. But what will the church do when it too becomes an acceptable form?

WHAT DOES THE BIBLE SAY?

"Let the word of Christ dwell in you richly in all wisdom; teaching and admonishing one another in psalms and hymns and spiritual songs, singing with grace in your hearts to the Lord" (Col. 3:16).

"Speaking to yourselves in psalms and hymns and spiritual songs, singing and making melody in your heart to the Lord; Giving thanks always for all things unto God and the Father in the name of our Lord Jesus Christ" (Eph. 5: 19, 20).

"And at midnight Paul and Silas prayed, and sang praises unto God: and the prisoners heard them" (Acts 16:25).

"What is it then? I will pray with the spirit, and I will pray with the understanding also: I will sing with the spirit, and I will sing with the understanding also" (I Cor. 14:15).

"And they sung a new song, saying, Thou art worthy to take the book, and to open the seals thereof: for thou wast slain, and hast redeemed us to God by thy blood out of every kindred, and tongue, and people, and nation" (Rev. 5:9).

"Is any among you afflicted? let him pray. Is any merry? let him sing psalms" (James 5: 13).

"O sing unto the Lord a new song; for he hath done marvellous things: his right hand, and his holy arm, hath gotten him the victory" (Ps. 98:1).

"Praise ye the Lord. Sing unto the Lord a new song, and his praise in the congregation of saints" (Ps. 149:1).

WHAT DO YOU SAY?

1. What is the implication of the psalmist's words to sing a "new" song? (Ps. 98:1, 149:1) Might it

include new musical expressions and forms? Why sing "new" songs?

2. What did the Apostle Paul mean when he spoke of singing in the spirit and with understanding? (I Cor. 14:15) Is this a guideline for church music today?

3. In the light of the apostles' custom of singing wherever they were (cf. Acts 16:25), and Paul's admonitions in Col. 3:16 and Eph. 5:19, 20, what is the fundamental purpose of hymn singing? If a song fulfils such a purpose, does that make it acceptable for Christian usage?

4. Does Paul's breakdown between "psalms, hymns, and spiritual songs" have any significance for us today? Doesn't this distinction implicitly affirm and justify the possibility of a wide variety of musical modes available to express our worship and spiritual feelings?

5. Is there such a thing as a "sacred" or "secular" musical style? If so, how are they differentiated?

6. Can a musical expression or style be evil in itself? Can a musical beat or tempo be immoral?

7. Is folk music an acceptable musical form for Christian worship? Should folk music be used in a morning worship service or only in young peoples' meetings? What is the difference between folk music and Negro spirituals?

8. Can jazz or other popular musical styles be incorporated into Christian worship? What artistic changes would be necessary if any? Would these forms of music need "cleansing" from a theological standpoint?

101

9. Should music in the church be chosen for its artistic and aesthetic value or for its spiritual content? Is using music for an emotional effect in church a proper motive?

10. In what ways do our present congregational hymnbooks need to be changed? How should hymns be revised or rewritten?

11. How can evangelicals inspire talented Christian people to write new hymns? What can be done to get them accepted by the Christian public? How can Christian music publishers help?

12. What value would there be in writing new words that reflected more of our times and culture to some of the familiar hymns and gospel song tunes? Or, should we try to revamp our hymnbooks completely by substituting modern songs?

Notes

1. Lawrence J. Richards, "18th and 19th Century Hymns for Always?" *United Evangelical Action,* November, 1967, p. 23. Used by permission of *United Evangelical Action,* official publication of the National Association of Evangelicals.

2. *Ibid.*

3. Don Hustad, "Where Are We Going in Church Music?" *Moody Monthly*, March, 1966, p. 21. Used by permission.

4. *Ibid.*

Are Urban Centers Lost to the Gospel? 12

AMERICAN CITIES seem to be facing problems which seem beyond solution. The revolution and unrest in the American city is our number one domestic issue. It includes almost all the racial and ecological problems of modern man: riots, air and water pollution, crime, poverty, vice, slum housing, unskilled labor, and congested transportation facilities. In fact, one can say that the big city breeds such problems and seems to have no way of keeping them from getting out of hand.

Up to this point, no governmental program designed to stop urban decay has made any substantial progress. Traditionally, the American mood has been anti-city. Americans have always glorified the open spaces and fresh air. The mark of success for many Americans has been the ability to purchase a home in the suburbs, thus fleeing the frustrations of city life. While one can hardly condemn the desire to better one's standard of living, the overall effect of the suburban sprawl has been to accelerate the problems of the central and inner city.

While the middle class moves to the suburbs, the disenfranchised poor, usually Negroes, move into the congested "urbania." While the new suburban dwellers are greeted by the "Welcome Wagon" and given every aid to adjust, the ghetto dwellers go unrecognized.

James M. Gavin and Arthur Hadly in *Saturday Review* make this point in an article, "The Crisis of the Cities": "The cities make new efforts to ease the entry of the new arrival. There are no special communities to receive the migrant, retrain him, place him in decent housing, find him a job. At this crucial moment of his life, when a whole complex of resources should be focused to aid him, he finds himself alone. Isolated, discriminated against, lacking the education, skills and knowledge necessary in a highly industrialized society, bewildered by his new environment, the migrant separates from the mainstream of America and joins the undercurrent — the underculture of poverty."[1]

It is the vastness of the problem that staggers social reformers and city planners. Between 1960 and 1970 it is estimated that nearly 10 million farmers alone will have migrated into American cities. This alone, not counting the larger population growth among non-whites already in the cities, will create many social problems. Add to these prejudices, congestion, discrimination, poverty, and unemployment and the situation seems to beget hopelessness.

Eighty percent of Americans live in cities and the figure grows daily. The population increase in urban centers creates a need for more space for meeting the growing demands. Urban centers are already overpopulated. Soon the sprawling cities will reach out into the comfortable suburbs to form great megalopolises.

The process of super urbanization seems to change the very significance of man. He is losing his importance by the necessity of conforming to big city life. He simply becomes one more item in the city's problems. As society operates more and more through mechanization, the individual — especially the unskilled worker — loses much of his identity. A kind of anonymity pervades much of city life and the individual soon loses his humanity. Along with this is a loss of a sense of individual worth, a sense of values, a compassionate interest in others, and a sense of community.

Cities are not only moving out; they are also moving up. Such a pattern also changes the patterns of living and the general outlook of the city dweller. High-rise housing projects were thought to be one of the best answers to replacing slum housing and providing middle-class housing. But the high-rise apartment presents problems perhaps unseen by the originators of such buildings. Lack of space, close proximity, a non-interest in neighbors — all these have created a new king of ghettos — the high-rise ghetto.

In the public housing high-rise buildings, little attention is given to the problems of the family with children who live on the upper floors. Playground space is impractical for a mother with small children when she lives on the 16th floor. She simply must keep her children boxed in with her.

Even the plush-type high-rise apartments have their effects on modern urban culture. It is common to live in such buildings for several years and never see your neighbors, much less become acquainted with them. It is possible never to see a mailman. The largest percent of the people who live in these vertical cities love the privacy and anonymity they afford. Each building becomes an anonymous community within itself, self-sufficient in every way. Many of these skyscrapers contain more people than do most small towns in America.

For better or for worse, urban renewal is even spelling the doom of the ubiquitous Skid Row that has plagued American cities. Between 1947 and 1967 the Bowery's population fell from 13,500 to 4,000 and it is declining at least 5% each year.

The exact meaning of all this urban change is not fully understood by modern man. It is really too different and perhaps too soon to predict the outcome. We just haven't had to face such forces of change and population growth before. Rising incomes, technology, the gap between the rich and the poor, changing social attitudes – these have clouded our perspective and directions.

What does all this mean to the evangelical Christian? Where does he fit in? How can he help? What is his role? Evangelicals, like most other middle-class people, have been caught off guard by our changing society. Many evangelicals have plainly ignored the problem, merely satisfied to support a few rescue missions so their men's fellowship can have an outlet for Christian service once a month.

Some evangelicals, however, are deeply concerned about the problems that our cities face. A recent issue of *United Evangelical Action* (Spring, 1968) carried an article, "Have Evangelicals Abandoned the Cities?" which emphasized the need for Christians to become involved in city problems and minister more effectively to its needs. It described the American cities as "one of the major mission responsibilities of the church's entire history."

Dr. Marvin K. Mayers, writing in the same issue of *Action*, expressed the real need. He said, "A few churches are holding 'the Word' in nearly impossible situations. Some are experimenting with new and radical types of evangelism, such as high-rise evangelism and coffee house ministries, and are having a limited, though encouraging, success. Community renewal programs are beginning to operate. Brave educators are holding fast to sound educational techniques suitable for work among a variety of ethnic groups that are part of every city's challenge.

"The magnitude of the task, however, demands more than just an isolated foray into the 'enemy's lines'; more than a brave stand against overwhelming odds. It demands a concerted attack by Christians in the church, working with our finest business and government leaders, to assure the following:

"That men might know Jesus Christ in a dynamic encounter.

"That there might be economic stability for each in his own sector of society.

"That whatever money is available be applied to the real need.

"That blood-related and interest groups might be able to grow and develop in an atmosphere of trust.

"That individuals may not be used as pawns in power plays, either economic, political or religious."[2]

Suburbia has been most Americans' answer to the urban dilemma. Leave the city to fend for itself. Empty and dwindling churches in the city are monuments to a general attitude among evangelicals to follow the crowd without making any plans to reach those who fill the inner city. Of course, one cannot expect the suburbanites to move back into the city — or can we? But some other approach must be considered by evangelicals who care about the problems of the city. Some Christians are now awakening to the fact that the problems cities now face will be their own problems within a few years when their little community takes on more and more of the big city characteristics.

Dr. Mayers suggests a "missionary approach" which would entail families or individuals taking residence in the heart of the big city and doing missionary work. He says, "Granted, it will not be easy to leave today's suburbia and transplant a family into the urban complex, but neither is it easy to do this when moving to Nigeria or New Guinea. There may need to be furloughs provided such people; even children's schools to insure them an adequate level of education, at least at first until the educational level of the local schools becomes adequate for all. Occupational activities should be sought within the local area if possible. What has happened to the average American evangelical, I'm afraid, is that he has taken the ways of the 'world' mentioned in Romans 12, e.g. obsession with our homes, our security programs, the level of our children's education. We are told rather, 'Don't copy the behavior and customs of this world, but be a new and different person with a fresh newness in all you do and think" (Living Letters). Perhaps we need to take a few risks for the sake of our wonderful Lord."[3]

Cities are people — many people who together make up a great mass of humanity for whom Christ died. Jesus wept over a great city. Jeremiah lamented the fall of the great city of Jerusalem. His words speak poignantly to us today, "Is it nothing to you all ye that pass by?" (Lam. 1:12). Perhaps it is time that evangelicals take a clearer look at the "multitudes" around them and get concerned and involved in a more personal way. After all, the call to the uttermost parts of the earth (Acts 1:8) is preceded by a call to stay in the city. Among the perils Paul mentioned in his ministry for Christ were the "perils in the cities" (II Cor. 11: 26). Working and living in our large urban centers does involve risk and peril. Perhaps more than foreign missionaries in other lands who are treated as guests.

WHAT DOES THE BIBLE SAY?

"And Jesus went about all the cities and villages, teaching in their synagogues, and preaching the gospel of the kingdom, and healing every sickness and every disease among the people" (Matt. 9:35).

"And it came to pass, when Jesus had made an end of commanding his twelve disciples, he departed thence to teach and to preach in their cities" (Matt. 11:1).

"And he said unto them, I must preach the kingdom of God to other cities also: for therefore am I sent" (Luke 4:43).

"But Philip was found at Azotus: and passing through he preached in all the cities, till he came to Caesarea." (Acts 8:40).

"In journeyings often, in perils of waters, in perils of robbers, in perils by mine own countrymen, in perils by the heathen, in perils in the city, in perils in the wilderness, in perils in the sea, in perils among false brethren" (II Cor. 11:26).

"But ye shall receive power, after that the Holy Ghost is come upon you: and ye shall be witnesses unto me both in Jerusalem, and in all Judea, and in Samaria, and unto the uttermost part of the earth" (Acts 1:8).

WHAT DO YOU SAY?

1. Should evangelical involvement in the needs of the inner city be limited to spiritual aspects of the problems? Why? or why not?

2. In what ways have evangelicals in the past pioneered in alleviating big city social problems? How effective have these programs been? Why have so many of them been abandoned?

3. What is the role of the rescue mission in the city? Should they be scrapped? Should they be changed? How can they be made more effective?

4. How can rescue missions meet the changing needs and character of the modern city?

5. How can suburban churches help inner city churches meet the problems of dwindling and changing memberships?

6. How should city churches in rapidly changing neighborhoods adapt to community needs? Should they simply move with the people?

7. Could cities be considered valid mission fields to which churches would actually send and support persons to minister? Would this effort be any less missionary work than in the Congo?

8. Home mission efforts seem oriented toward rural, suburban, and smaller minority groups. Should our home mission board place more emphasis upon supporting pastors in the inner city or work with families to live and witness in high rises?

9. What steps can your local church take to strengthen evangelical witnesses in our big cities?

10. What methods of evangelism can be devised to reach the people in high-rise apartments where traditional door-to-door methods are impossible? How can the church penetrate these communities?

Notes

1. James M. Gavin and Arthur Hadley, "The Crisis of the Cities." *Saturday Review*, February 24, 1968, p. 31. Used by permission.

2. Marvin K. Mayers, "Have Evangelicals Abandoned the Cities?" *United Evangelical Action*, Spring, 1968. Used by permission of *United Evangelical Action*, official publication of the National Association of Evangelicals.

13 Our Country: Right or Wrong?

A 19TH-CENTURY American naval officer named Stephen Decatur is credited with the words, "Our country! In her intercourse with foreign nations may she be always right; but our country, right or wrong."

This is no doubt a very patriotic statement, borne out of an intense loyalty to one's country. But it certainly raises some questions. What would happen if we would take such a statement and put it in the mouth of a member of the German high command during Hitler's reign of terror? Intense patriotism was a vital part of Germany's loyalty to the Third Reich during World War II.

Looking back on history and taking into account some of the atrocities committed by the Nazis, one would find it hard to justify such a sentiment — especially from the lips of a Christian. Yet there are some Christians who have made patriotism synonymous with religious zeal. They almost view patriotism as one of the fruits of the Spirit. "God and country" to them are inseparable concepts.

Their reasoning is rather simple. God helped the founding fathers set up this land. God has blessed America. Therefore God is on our side and to oppose the policies of our nation is to fight against God. To be loyal to God, we must be loyal to America right or wrong; we must defend her in all her actions. We must preserve and conserve the freedoms for which we fought. Right or wrong we must defend our country. The assumption, however, is that because God is on our side we can never really be wrong.

Not all Christians share such views. They can point out that Adolph Hitler thought God was on his side too. Kent D. Moorehead, writing in *Together,* said: "The cry, 'my country right or wrong' is nonsense. That is like saying, 'My water fresh or poisoned.' The statement 'My country right or wrong' is often used as a blanket endorsement of our nation's policies, and yet it can pave the way for a fascist state. A better statement was made by Carl Schurz, 19th century reformer: 'Our country, right or wrong! When right, to be kept right: when wrong to be put right!'"[1]

Most Christian people would endorse a patriotic attitude as a necessary duty of citizenship. The question, however, comes as to how far to carry a patriotic spirit. Does Christian patriotism blind one to the faults of his country's policies? Is his patriotism a substitute for effective witness to the world? Can patriotism itself be an idolatry for Christians committed to the cause of Jesus Christ?

Others feel that the primary task of the believer is to be a witness of the resurrection of Christ and not to be entangled in patriotic zealotry.

"Our commission is not to further the American way of life or maintain the status quo in the balance of power, but to hold true to the revealed Word of God and proclaim its message to the world. We are not called to be anti-Communists or anti-anything else. We are to be ambassadors for Christ, and to the extent that we have lost this vision we are failing miserably in our task."[2]

The Christian must ask at what point does loyalty to country end and loyalty to God begin. Especially when his country espouses a policy or action that is contrary to God's law. The Christian must be willing to scrutinize his country's action in the light of God's revealed will. At this point many Christian people fail to bring biblical principles into honest dialogue with their nationalistic policies. "It is not acceptable to adopt the nationalistic slogans of the day under the guise of Christian patriotism . . . May we have the courage to search through the issues of the day and speak out as our consciences direct, for only as God's people seek His face and do His will may a nation receive His favor."[3] Loyalty to the state is conditioned by loyalty to God, not the other way around.

When Christians consider their patriotic duties they need to find a sane and balanced position. It is no sin for Christians to be active in politics or to pledge allegiance to their flag. Perhaps too many Christians sin by their inaction rather than their over-action. The Apostle Paul accepted and took advantage of his Roman citizenship, but he was not a slave to the state. Peter urged Christians to obey "every ordinance of man for the Lord's sake" (I Peter 2:13, 14), but obeyed God rather than men (Acts 4:19, 20; Acts 5:29) when man's rules vitiated God's will. Paul (Romans 13) made it clear that Christians are expected to be responsible citizens toward the state and even to pray for its leaders (I Tim. 2). Does this mean that we should be uncritically compliant when our government acts irresponsibly?

Irresponsible governmental action and Christian responsibility to speak against such action become more viable issues in a country that claims God's favor. Perhaps Christian response might differ toward a state antagonistic toward religion.

Paul seems to imply in Romans 13 that our responsibility is to responsible government. Rulers are looked upon as "terrors" toward evil, who "praise" good deeds (v. 3); and who stand in judgment on evil doers (v. 4). The assumption is that the government itself is based on laws and principles of justice.

Hudson T. Armerding, president of Wheaton College, says ". . . the government in question in Romans 13 is one which is a government of laws which acts in such a fashion as to exhibit a responsibility to God as well as to man and which demonstrates this in a practical way through the support of the good and the punishment of the evil as these terms are defined in the Scripture. A government which does not fulfil these stipulations presumably is acting counter to the will of God and merits His judgment. In such a case should it have the active patriotic support of God's people?"[4]

Many Christians today do not feel that the United States is following just policies. They feel America's involvement in the Viet Nam war is illegal and immoral. From the beginning it required funds that should have been slated toward social legislation at home to alleviate the misery and poverty of millions who live in our city ghettos. They think America's "policing" of the world is imperialistic, and that our opposition to seating Red China in the United Nations is wrong. Perhaps these attitudes are oversimplified, but they are enough to create a credibility gap and influence many Christians to speak out against United States foreign policy. Many American Christians, who love their country deeply are seriously concerned about some of its actions. To make their concerns known they have even made statements that have jeopardized their standing with other Christians. Yet they have had courage to speak according to their conscience.

Some Christians in the name of patriotism have felt that extremism used to defend our liberties is justified. They arduously defended Barry Goldwater's famous statement during the 1964 presidential campaign that "extremism in the defense of liberty is no vice". Others, however, feel that it is really a matter of priorities and balance. Hudson Armerding said, ". . . we can properly be actively Christian and at the same time actively patriotic. We should maintain this practice as long as in our opinion the government of the United States, through its constitutional form and its system of jurisprudence, continues to act in a manner consistent with those principles set forth in Romans 13. In so doing we recognize that our highest loyalty is 'for Christ and His Kingdom.' "[5]

But what divides our nation at present is our inability to determine whether the actions of the United States are in line with moral law and with scriptural principles. Both Christians and non-Christians ask whether America is right in spending billions to get to the moon, when 22 million people are in poverty. Is America right in fighting wars that not only waste billions of dollars, but cost precious lives abroad and stifle social progress at home? Is America right in developing missile systems that accelerate an arms race around the world, bringing the world closer to potential annihilation? Or does our patriotism simply lead us into an arrogant indifference about such questions, forcing us to preserve our national honor rather than our Christian conscience?

116

WHAT DOES THE BIBLE SAY?

"Submit yourselves to every ordinance of man for the Lord's sake: whether it be to the king, as supreme; or unto governors, as unto them that are sent by him for the punishment of evildoers, and for the praise of them that do well. For so is the will of God, that with well-doing ye may put to silence the ignorance of foolish men: As free, and not using your liberty for a cloak of maliciousness, but as the servants of God. Honor all men. Love the brotherhood. Fear God. Honor the king" (I Peter 2:13-17).

"Let every soul be subject unto the higher powers. For there is no power but of God: the powers that be are ordained of God. Whosoever, therefore, resisteth the power, resisteth the ordinance of God; and they that resist shall receive to themselves damnation. For rulers are not a terror to good works, but to the evil. Wilt thou then not be afraid of the power? do that which is good, and thou shalt have praise of the same: For he is the minister of God to thee for good. But if thou do that which is evil, be afraid; for he beareth not the sword in vain: for he is the minister of God, a revenger to execute wrath upon him that doeth evil. Wherefore ye must needs be subject, not only for wrath, but also for conscience' sake" (Rom. 13:1-5).

"Put them in mind to be subject to principalities and powers, to obey magistrates, to be ready to every good work" (Titus 3:1).

"For our citizenship is in heaven; whence also we wait for a Savior, the Lord Jesus Christ" (Phil. 3:20).

"They say unto him, Caesar's. Then saith he unto them, Render therefore unto Caesar the things which are Caesar's; and unto God the things that are God's" (Matt. 22:21).

"Jesus answered, Thou couldest have no power at all against me, except it were given thee from above: therefore he that delivered me unto thee hath the greater sin" (John 19:11).

WHAT DO YOU SAY?

1. Can we assume that when a government does not fulfil the stipulations of Romans 13 that Christians have the right to oppose its actions? Or should Christians follow the dictates of whatever government they are under?

2. Why do many assume that our American republic and democratic form of government is Christian? Is it? Is there a specifically "Christian" form of government?

3. What are the implications of our dual citizenship (Philippians 3:20) toward God and man? Should a Christian renounce his earthly roots and national loyalties?

4. What are the implications of Paul's appeal to his Roman citizenship to guarantee a civil right? (Acts 22:25-29)

5. Are Christian anti-communist efforts supported by Scripture? How do they relate to the Christian mandate to take the gospel to all the world?

6. When, if ever, is the statement, "My country, right or wrong" a valid one? Can a Christian make that statement?

7. Some of Jesus' disciples confused the redemptive mission of Christ with their messianic nationalism (Acts 1:6). Are there Christians today who similarly confuse the redemptive message of the gospel with their political activism and zealous patriotism? How do they evidence this confusion?

8. To what extent should a Christian practice patriotism? Is patriotism a Christian virtue? If so, how should it be expressed? How can we avoid the pitfalls of being overly patriotic?

9. Can an American who holds a liberal or progressive political philosophy truly be patriotic? Or does one have to be a political conservative to be a true patriot?

10. Would you consider the late Norman Thomas or the late Senator Joseph McCarthy patriotic Americans? How did their political views differ?

11. What elements of our national policies (foreign or domestic) should cause Christians to speak out for definite and even drastic changes? How should Christians express their dissatisfaction or opposition?

Notes

1. From the article "Obey God — Or Men?" by Kent D. Moorehead, *Together*, November, 1968, p. 27. Used by permission of The Methodist Publishing House.

2. Emery J. Cummins, "My Country: Right or Wrong," *Eternity Magazine,* June, 1967, p. 30. Used by permission of *Eternity Magazine.*

3. *Ibid,* p. 38.

4. Hudson T. Armerding, "Is Patriotism Christian?" *United Evangelical Action,* July, 1966, p. 6. Used by permission of *United Evangelical Action,* official publication of the National Association of Evangelicals.

5. *Ibid.,* p. 14.